I0426716

ENGAGE:
Content Marketing Magic For Women In Business

By Donna-Marie Coggins

ISBN: 9798876576026

Disclaimer

The Author and Publisher have strived to be as accurate and complete as possible in the creation of this book, notwithstanding the fact that they do not warrant or represent at any time that the contents within are accurate due to the rapidly changing nature of the Internet.

While all attempts have been made to verify information provided in this publication, the Author and Publisher assume no responsibility for errors, omissions, or contrary interpretation of the subject matter herein.

In practical books, like anything else in life, there are no guarantees. Readers are cautioned to rely on their own judgment about their individual circumstances and to act accordingly.

This book is not intended for use as a source of legal, business, accounting or financial advice. All readers are advised to seek services of competent professionals in each relevant field.

DEDICATION

To the spirited solopreneurs, the courageous women embarking on their entrepreneurial journeys... this book is dedicated to you, my beautiful friends. May it be a beacon of enchantment and inspiration, guiding you through a world brimming with magic and possibility. In these pages, find the strength to weave your dreams into reality and the courage to transform challenges into stepping-stones on your path to success.

And to Anthony, whose support, encouragement and love have been my unwavering foundation: may my books inspire you to find your tribe and pursue all that brings you joy, in the same way as you have always inspired me.

Other Books By Donna-Marie Coggins:

As you turn the pages of this book, remember it's the beginning of an incredible journey. This is the first of a series of books crafted by Donna-Marie Coggins, each book a stepping stone on your path to crafting a business and life by your own design. Imagine a world where you are the author of your own story, where every challenge is a plot twist leading to personal growth and business success. That's the world these books aim to help you create.

To continue this adventure together, and to be the first to know about the latest books as they're lovingly brought to life, visit **www.Donna-MarieCoggins.com/dm-books**. Picture each book as a new chapter in your entrepreneurial journey, filled with insights, inspiration and the kind of practical guidance that can only come from someone who walks the walk.

Let's turn dreams into plans and plans into the kind of success stories that you'll one day share with others. Because in this community, we don't just dream; we do.

Contents

A Personal Message From The Author ~ Donna-Marie Coggins

Hello Gorgeous Reader,

As you turn these pages, I want you to feel as though we're old friends catching up over a cup of coffee *(or your favourite drink!)*. This book is a heartfelt conversation between you and me, a shared journey into the world of entrepreneurship, tailored especially for women who are travelling on this exciting, sometimes daunting, path of being a solopreneur.

While this book was written with a focus on women, using language that reflects our unique experiences in the business world, the strategies and insights shared are universal. Whether you identify as a woman or not, the information contained within these pages can be a powerful tool in anyone's entrepreneurial arsenal.

Embarking on this journey won't always be easy. You'll encounter challenges and there will be times when things don't go as planned. Remember, it's perfectly okay not to get everything right from the start. I've been in this field for many years and I'm still adapting every day. But I know it's okay. The key is to begin. Take that first step... and then build upon it, step-by-step, layer-by-layer. Your business, like this book, is a journey – not a destination.

I want this book to be a source of inspiration and guidance, a magical and enchanting guide that lifts you up and helps you navigate the often-complex world of content marketing. So, find your coziest reading spot, grab your favourite beverage, and let's dive into this adventure together. Here's to your success, your growth and the fabulous journey ahead!

With much warmth and encouragement,
Donna-Marie xo

Chapter 1: Introduction

Crafting Your Content Journey

Welcome, my beautiful friend! Get ready to sink into the coziness of your favourite reading spot because we're about to explore the fascinating world of content marketing. This isn't only about marketing; it's about creating a symphony of engagement, connection and resonance.

So, let's unfold the layers and delve deeper into the magic of crafting your content journey.

The Power of Content Marketing

A Symphony of Engagement
Imagine your business is a symphony, each piece of content a note that contributes to the harmonious composition. Content marketing is the conductor, guiding each element to create a melody that resonates with your audience.

It's not merely about providing information; it's about creating an experience, a journey that your audience willingly takes with you.

Shifting Tides in Consumer Behaviour
We're witnessing a shift in consumer behaviour. Traditional advertising, with its one-way communication, is losing its effectiveness.

Consumers are actively seeking authenticity, connection and value.

In fact, studies show that nearly 90% of consumers find custom content useful and more than 75% prefer it over traditional advertising. The power dynamic has shifted; your audience wants to be engaged, not sold to.

The Human Touch

For small business owners, this shift is a golden opportunity. Your authentic voice, your unique perspective and your personal touch become the distinguishing factors.

No longer do you need to try to fit in with the traditional forms of advertising. Now, you can be your beautiful self. Let your uniqueness shine and attract those who are best suited for you and your business.

Your audience isn't just buying a product or service; they're investing in a relationship with you. The great news is, content marketing allows you to humanise your brand, making it relatable, trustworthy and appealing.

The Landscape of Modern Business

Stats Speak Louder Than Words

Here are some eye-opening statistics to consider:

- Over 70% of consumers prefer getting to know a company through articles rather than ads.
- Businesses that prioritise blogging are 13 times more likely to see a positive return on investment *(ROI)*.
- Approximately 60% of consumers feel more positive about a company after reading custom content on its site.

These numbers tell a compelling story, don't you think?

Content marketing isn't a mere trend; it's a fundamental shift in how businesses connect with their audience. And if you're not doing it – or not doing it right – you may soon be left in the wake of your competition *(if you're not already)*.

Beyond the Transaction

Your business is more than a transaction; it's an ongoing conversation.

Content marketing is the language you use to communicate your brand's story, values and mission. It's about creating a narrative that goes beyond the features of your product or service and even beyond the basic benefit. It taps into the emotions and aspirations of your audience.

Why This Matters For Entrepreneurs

The Power of Your Voice

The world needs to hear your voice. Small business owners bring a unique perspective, a different energy to the business landscape.
Studies consistently show that diversity in leadership, leads to better business outcomes. Content marketing becomes the amplifier for your voice, allowing you to resonate in a way that stands out amidst the noise.

Navigating the Sea of Businesses

In a market saturated with options, your authenticity becomes your beacon. Content marketing positions you as more than a provider. It establishes you as a thought leader... a guide... and a trusted ally in your customer's journey.

The Essence of Content Marketing

A Two-Way Street

Content marketing is a dynamic, two-way street. It's not just about broadcasting your message; it's about actively engaging with your audience. This engagement isn't a one-time affair; it's an ongoing relationship-building process.

Content as a Conversation Starter

Imagine your business as a cozy coffee shop and your content as the friendly conversation starter. It's the initial handshake, the warm greeting that invites your audience to sit down and connect. Content marketing facilitates this conversation on a digital platform, making it accessible to a broader audience.

Here's a great analogy I like to use when teaching content marketing...

If you were to see someone you thought looked nice, would you go up to them and ask them to marry you?

I expect not. *(And if you do, there may be some other issues to address here!)*

That would be creepy. The usual process is to have a two-way conversation with the person first. Then, all going well for you both, you might exchange contact details and arrange to get together later, maybe for dinner or a drink.

Then you continue to engage with each other and get to know each other better. You may discover you're a perfect match and decide to get married and live happily ever after. Or you may decide to part ways. Or to keep in touch as friends, but nothing more. But it all starts by getting a better understanding of each other and each other's needs first, right?

Content marketing takes your potential customers on a similar sort of journey. Potential customers, or prospects, see your content and choose to engage with you in some way. You continue to build a relationship with them to get to know each other better and find out if your product or service is a good solution for them.

Eventually, they may buy from you. Or they *(or you)* may decide you're not a good fit and they continue looking elsewhere.

However, trying to get someone who sees your business, product or service for the first time to buy from you, before you've even had a chance to know if your product or service is right for them, is like proposing to someone you don't yet even know.

The Variety of Content

Beyond Text: The Multifaceted Approach

Content comes in various forms and each format serves a unique purpose. For example, blog posts provide in-depth information, podcasts offer a personal touch, videos create visual narratives and social media fosters real-time connections.

Creating different types of content and on different platforms ensures that you're catering to different preferences within your audience.

Statistics on Format Effectiveness

Did you know...?

- Video content on social media generates 12 times more shares than text and images combined.
- Blogs are rated as the fifth most trusted source for accurate online information.
- Podcast listeners are highly engaged, with 80% listening to all or most of each episode.

Understanding the strengths of each format empowers you to craft a holistic content strategy. But that's not the only thing to consider, so keep reading for the full picture.

The Social Media Symphony

The Pinnacle of Connectivity

Social media is more than a platform; it's a cultural phenomenon. It's where conversations happen, trends emerge and connections flourish. Harnessing the power of social media is not only beneficial; it may be imperative for the modern entrepreneur.

But we need to keep in mind that social media isn't all roses. There are some downfalls that trap many an unsuspecting person. More on this later.

The Global Playground

Think of social media as a global playground where your audience gathers. With over 3.6 billion active users, it's a landscape where your brand can create a resonance that reverberates across borders.

Social Media Mastery

Mastering social media involves understanding each platform's nuances, leveraging visual storytelling and embracing real-time engagement. More importantly than posting, it's about participating in the ongoing dialogue.

Crafting Your Content Journey

As we venture deeper into this book, we're going deeper than exploring content marketing strategies; we're co-creating a roadmap for your unique content journey.

We'll uncover the secrets of effective storytelling, explore practical strategies for different content formats and infuse a sprinkle of mindset magic because, my friend, your mindset is the secret sauce that makes it all come together.

So... are you ready to transform your business into a content-driven powerhouse?

I thought so. Let's take another sip and let the content adventure continue!

PART 1:
FOUNDATIONS

Welcome to **PART 1: FOUNDATIONS**. This section sets the stage for your content marketing journey – it's all about creating a rock-solid groundwork to support your success.

Now, I get it; planning might not be the most glamourous part of the process, but trust me, it's absolutely essential. Think of it as having a clear roadmap for your journey. It makes everything smoother and less overwhelming.

In the Foundations section, we're going to begin by shining a spotlight on YOU – your business, your identity.

- *Who are you at your core?*
- *What do you stand for?*
- *What are your goals and aspirations?*
- *Who are the amazing people you're here to serve?*
- *And what unique problems do you solve for them?*
- *Oh, and let's not forget your brand – what sets you apart and makes you unforgettable?*

But it doesn't stop there. We'll also embark on a journey of discovery to truly understand your market – the people who will be hanging onto your every word. The better you know them, the more they'll feel like you're speaking directly to them, addressing their unique challenges and aspirations.

And you know what happens when people feel understood? They're more likely to become your raving fans and loyal customers.

So, my friend, let's roll up our sleeves and start building the unshakable foundations that will set the stage for your content marketing triumphs!

Chapter 2: Discovering Your Brand Story

Uncovering the Unique Narrative That Sets Your Business Apart and Resonates with Your Audience

Hello again, my fellow adventurer! I'm excited you've returned for another chapter of our exploration into the enchanting world of content marketing.

So, settle into your most comfortable seat, get that tea steeping and let's start out on the art of discovering your brand story – a narrative that doesn't tell, but instead sings to the hearts of your audience, setting your business apart and forming a deep, resonant connection.

The Power of Storytelling

Your Business, Your Epic

Picture this: your business is not merely a series of transactions. It's an epic tale waiting to be told.

Your journey as an entrepreneur is filled with twists, turns, challenges and triumphs, forming the very essence of your brand. This narrative is not only about marketing; it's the soul of your business. It's about going above the transactional and inviting your audience into a captivating journey.

The Emotional Connection

Before we dive deeper, let's acknowledge the profound impact of storytelling on human emotions. Stories, when crafted with care, have the power to resonate on a deep, emotional level.

Consider this: studies show that emotions heavily influence consumer decision-making. When your audience connects emotionally with your brand story, they're doing more than purchasing a product. They're investing in an experience, a journey and a piece of your narrative.

Unveiling Your Brand Essence

Beyond Features and Benefits

Now, let's peel back the layers and explore the essence of your brand. It's more than the tangible features and benefits of your product or service. It's the intangible elements that create a distinctive flavour, a unique identity.

It's about uncovering what makes your brand truly special... the secret sauce that sets you apart from the competition.

Identifying Core Values

Central to your brand essence are your core values – the guiding principles that shape your business decisions. These values are not just for show. They're the heartbeat of your brand.

For example, my brand's values include:

- Honesty and transparency
- Kindness, respect, genuinely helping others and lifting each other up
- Family
- Health
- Freedom *(including the freedom to make our own choices, to allow ourselves permission to want what we want, to live life on our terms and to have financial freedom.)*

Let's take a moment for introspection.

What values matter most to you?

How do these values align with the needs and aspirations of your audience?

Identifying and embracing these values will be the compass for your brand story.

Crafting a Mission Statement

Your mission statement is more than a formality; it's the rallying cry, the declaration of purpose that guides your business journey. Crafting a compelling mission statement involves distilling your business' impact, the change you want to bring and the legacy you aim to leave.

It's more than a string of words; it's the North Star that keeps your brand on course, shaping the narrative for both your team and your audience.

Your Personal Journey

The Entrepreneurial Odyssey

Your journey as an entrepreneur is a story in itself – a narrative of resilience, growth and self-discovery.

Your audience wants to connect with the human side of your business. Share the challenges you've overcome, the lessons you've learned and the victories you've celebrated. Your personal journey humanises your brand, making it relatable and creating a connection with your audience.

Overcoming Challenges

Don't shy away from shining a light on the challenges you've faced. Trust me, your audience doesn't expect perfection. What they crave authenticity.

When you share how you navigated obstacles, you not only showcase resilience but also provide inspiration for others facing similar challenges.

Vulnerability in storytelling fosters a genuine connection, as it shows that you're more than a business owner; you're a fellow traveller on the road of entrepreneurship.

Celebrating Milestones

On the flip side, celebrate your victories!

Whether it's reaching a significant sales milestone, launching a new product or receiving glowing testimonials, these moments are integral to your brand story.

They showcase progress, growth, and the positive impact your business has on your customers. The celebration isn't only about the achievement or seeking attention – it's about the shared joy with your audience.

Crafting Your Origin Story

The Beginning

Every superhero has an origin story and so does your brand. Your origin story is the opening chapter, the foundation upon which your business narrative is built.

Where did it all begin?
What inspired you to start this journey?

Your origin story is a captivating narrative that invites your audience into the genesis of your business, forging a connection from the very start.

The Spark of Inspiration

Share the moment of inspiration that led to the birth of your business.

Was it a personal experience, a problem you encountered or a passion that ignited your entrepreneurial spirit?

When your audience understands the beginning, they connect with the why behind your business. This emotional connection forms a strong bond, as they see the authentic spark that sets your entrepreneurial journey ablaze.

Introducing Your Team

If you have a team, introduce them through your origin story. Highlight their roles, contributions and the shared vision that unites your collective efforts.

The people behind your brand add depth and personality to your narrative. Introducing your team fosters a sense of community and shared purpose, showing that your brand story is a collective journey, rather than being about individuals.

The Language of Your Brand

Finding Your Tone

As every story has a unique tone, your brand has a language of its own.

Are you casual and conversational, formal and professional, or perhaps a mix of both?

Mostly, I use a friendly, conversational and engaging tone. I write and speak as if I'm speaking with my friends, because that's how I consider those who invest their time to consume my content.

I tend to refer to people as 'Lovely', 'Gorgeous', 'my beautiful friend', 'content rockstar' and other similar terms. Some people may not like this, but that's okay. My 'tribe'... my ideal clients, they're okay with this. Often, these are the sorts of words they use, too. And the common use of these words is one of the ways we relate with each other.

Your tone sets the stage for how your brand communicates with the world. Consider the preferences of your audience and the vibe that aligns with your brand essence. The tone should resonate with your audience, making them feel comfortable and engaged.

The Visual Narrative

Words paint a picture and visuals enhance that canvas. Your visual elements – logo, colour palette, imagery – contribute to the visual narrative of your brand story. Each element should harmonise with your brand essence, creating a cohesive and memorable brand identity. Visual consistency reinforces brand recognition, making your brand instantly recognisable across various platforms.

The Evolution of Your Brand

Embracing Change

As characters evolve in a story, your brand will go through transformations. Embrace change as a natural part of your business journey.

Whether it's a rebrand, a shift in focus or the introduction of new products, each chapter adds depth to your brand story. The ability to adapt signals resilience and relevance, showcasing that your brand is dynamic and responsive to the evolving needs of your audience.

At the time of writing this book, my business is going through a rebrand. I began my business in the late 1990s and it's had a few transitions since then! The business evolved... and I evolved. So, the brand is now evolving to keep up with the growth of myself and the business. :-)

Updating Your Narrative

As your business grows, your brand story may need updates too. Ensure that your narrative remains aligned with your current mission, values and goals. This doesn't mean discarding the past; it means evolving your story to reflect the present and future of your brand.

Consistent storytelling across different phases builds a narrative thread, allowing your audience to trace the evolution of your brand.

Making Your Brand Story Accessible
Storytelling Platforms

Now that you've unearthed the gems of your brand story, it's time to share it with the world. Consider the platforms where your audience engages the most. Whether it's your website, social media, newsletters or a combination of these, strategically place elements of your brand story where they will have the most impact. Each platform has its unique strengths; choose wisely based on your audience's preferences. *(We'll cover social media platforms and which ones you should be using in a later chapter.)*

Serialised Storytelling

Consider sharing your brand story in instalments. Like a captivating TV series keeps viewers hooked, revealing your brand story in episodes maintains your audience's interest.

Each instalment can delve into different aspects of your journey, creating anticipation for the next chapter. Serialised storytelling builds a sense of continuity, keeping your audience engaged over an extended period.

Case Studies: Brand Storytelling in Action

Toms: A Story of Impact

Now, let's dive into real-world examples of brand storytelling. Take Toms, for instance. This shoe company seamlessly integrates its mission into its brand story.

Founded on the principle of giving, Toms pledges to donate a pair of shoes for every pair sold. This narrative of impact creates a powerful connection between the brand and its audience. The story isn't about shoes; it's about making a difference and customers become part of that impact.

Nike: Empowering through Storytelling

Another great example is Nike, a brand synonymous with empowerment. Nike uses storytelling to inspire its audience.

Through powerful ads and campaigns, Nike weaves narratives of athletes overcoming challenges, pushing boundaries and achieving greatness. The brand's storytelling aligns with its core values, fostering a deep emotional connection with its audience.

Nike's brand story isn't about sports; it's about the spirit of relentless pursuit and customers become part of that journey.

That's so powerful.

Crafting Your Brand Story: A Personal Invitation

Reflection Questions

Before we wrap up this chapter, let's dig a little deeper in our exploration with some reflective questions:

- *What specific experiences or challenges in your personal journey as an entrepreneur have shaped your brand?*
- *How do your core values align with the needs and aspirations of your audience?*
- *Can you pinpoint a pivotal moment or experience that profoundly influenced your business?*
- *How do you celebrate victories, both big and small, in your business?*
- *What language and tone best reflect the personality of your brand?*

Next Steps

Armed with your reflections, consider the next steps in crafting and sharing your brand story:

- **Outline the Key Elements:** Choose the main elements you want to include in your brand story.
- **Identify Storytelling Platforms:** Determine the platforms where your audience is most receptive to storytelling.
- **Start Crafting Instalments:** Begin crafting your brand story in instalments, maintaining a consistent and engaging narrative.

Congratulations! You've taken your first steps on the journey of discovering your brand story! Well done, YOU!

In the next chapter, we'll explore practical strategies to nail your niche. The better you can show your audience that you know them, the more likely they are to resonate with you. But to do that, you need to really understand them – their problems and their desires. So, take a moment, reflect on your brand's essence and get ready for the next leg of our content adventure!

Chapter 3: Nailing Your Niche: Targeted Content For Your SPECIFIC Market

Understanding the Power of Niche Content and Tailoring Your Message for Your Specific Audience

Hello once again, Lovely! Get ready to dive deep into the magical world of content marketing in this chapter.

We're about to unravel the secrets of creating content that not only resonates but captivates your specific audience. So, grab your favourite cozy blanket and settle in – it's time to master the art of nailing your niche.

The Essence of Niche Content

Going Beyond Generalities

Let's shatter a common myth: the one-size-fits-all approach to content marketing. In the vast expanse of the internet, where attention is a precious commodity and competition is relentless, generic content often gets lost in the cacophony. This is where niche content emerges as your superhero cape, cutting through the noise to reach the hearts and minds of your specific audience.

Defining Your Niche

So, what exactly is a niche? Your niche is your sweet spot – the specific segment of the market that yearns for what you uniquely offer.

It's not about what you sell. It's about who you sell it to and why they need it. Imagine you're a fitness coach. Your niche isn't "everyone who wants to get fit." Instead, it could be "busy mums looking for quick, effective home workouts."

See the difference?

That's the power of defining your niche. And when you know who your specific market is, you can tailor your products, service, branding and content to them.

When people in this niche get the feeling that you truly know them and understand what they need – and how and why they need it – they're more likely to buy from you.

The Benefits of Niche Content

There are so many benefits of niche content, including:

1. Connection and Trust

Niche content fosters a sense of community. When your audience feels like your content speaks directly to them, it builds trust and a stronger connection.

2. Expert Status

Positioning yourself as the go-to expert in a specific niche elevates your authority. Your audience sees you as the ultimate source for their needs.

3. Increased Engagement

Niche content tends to generate more engagement. Your audience is more likely to comment, share and participate when they feel the content is tailor-made for them.

4. Higher Conversion Rates

Tailoring your content to a specific audience increases the likelihood of converting leads into customers. Your message resonates because it directly addresses their pain points and desires.

5. Brand Loyalty

Niche content builds a tribe of loyal followers. When you consistently deliver content that speaks to their specific interests, your audience becomes not just customers but brand advocates.

Understanding Your Specific Audience

Creating Buyer Personas

Before you can nail your niche, you need to intimately understand your specific audience.

This involves creating detailed buyer personas. Think of buyer personas as your content's North Star – they guide your every move.

Dive deep into the demographics, psychographics, challenges and aspirations of your ideal customers. Are they Susan, the aspiring entrepreneur juggling family and business? Or maybe Jake, the tech-savvy professional seeking innovative solutions?

Empathy Mapping

To truly connect with your audience, you need to step into their shoes. That's where empathy mapping comes in.

Picture yourself as your audience and map out their feelings, thoughts and actions at every stage of their journey.

- *What keeps them up at night?*
- *What are they looking for and how will this benefit them?*
- *What brings them joy?*

Don't be afraid to dig deep here. Don't stop at 'they want to lose weight'. Yeah, perhaps they do. But **WHY** do they want to lose weight? What will that allow them to do, or stop doing? How do they feel now? How will they feel after you've helped them to solve this problem?

Understanding their emotions is the key to creating content that resonates on a profound level.

Analysing Customer Feedback

Customer feedback is a goldmine of insights – one that's too often overlooked.

Leverage surveys, reviews and direct feedback to understand the nuances of your audience's preferences.

- *What content do they find most valuable?*
- *What improvements do they suggest?*

Actively listening to your audience helps you refine your content strategy continually.

Tailoring Your Content to Your Niche

Content Formats That Resonate

Different types of content are valuable at different stages of your prospect's buying journey. For example, someone who's realising they may have a problem need content to help them become aware of exactly what problem they have.

Whereas someone who's aware of their problem and has evaluated their possible solutions is looking for content that helps them choose the product or service they're going to buy.

As well as this, different people will prefer content in different formats. So, it's important to include a variety of content types.

Here's a quick summary on some of the main content formats:

1. *Blogs and Articles*

Ideal for providing in-depth information and establishing thought leadership. Dive into detailed guides, case studies and industry insights. Videos, podcasts and other content can also be shared via your blog.

2. *Podcasts*

Great for auditory learners and those on the go. Perfect for interviews, discussions and storytelling. Bring in industry experts or share success stories.

3. *Videos*

Engaging and versatile. Use videos for tutorials, behind-the-scenes and personal messages. Show the human side of your brand.

4. Infographics

Ideal for visual learners. Condense complex information into visually appealing graphics. Create infographics that simplify industry trends or showcase data.

5. Webinars

Perfect for in-depth discussions, workshops and engaging with your audience in real-time. Host webinars on topics directly addressing your audience's challenges.

Crafting Content With a Purpose

1. Educational Content

Address pain points and provide solutions. Position yourself as the expert solving your prospects' problems. Create comprehensive guides and how-to content.

2. Inspirational Content

Share success stories, personal experiences and motivational content to uplift and inspire. Connect emotionally with your audience.

3. Entertaining Content

Inject humour and personality into your content. Make your audience look forward to your next piece. Share anecdotes, behind-the-scenes or industry-related jokes.

4. Interactive Content

Polls, quizzes and interactive elements enhance engagement and make your content more shareable. Create interactive content that allows your audience to participate.

The Power of Personalisation

Personalisation is an incredibly powerful way to help you connect with your audience. Doesn't it feel good when someone is speaking with you and they use your name or information to show that they're speaking directly to you?

Here are some ways to incorporate personalisation in your content:

1. Email Marketing

Tailor your email campaigns based on the preferences and behaviours of your audience. Segment your email list for personalised communication.

2. Personalised Recommendations

Leverage data to offer personalised product or service recommendations. Netflix's recommendation engine is a stellar example. Provide tailored suggestions based on the person's past interactions.

3. Dynamic Content on Websites

Customise website content based on user behaviour, creating a more personalised user experience. Use dynamic content modules to show relevant information based on their past interactions.

Examples of Niche Content Done Right

An excellent example of niche content done right is Dove's Real Beauty Campaign. Dove carved a niche by challenging beauty stereotypes. Their content focuses on body positivity, diversity and self-love, resonating with a specific audience tired of unrealistic beauty standards. They feature real people with diverse body types in their campaigns.

Another good example of niche content is Buffer: Social Media for Small Businesses. Buffer's niche is clear: small businesses navigating the world of social media. Their content provides practical tips, case studies and resources tailored to the specific needs of small business owners. They offer social media strategies that cater to the challenges faced by smaller enterprises.

Blue Apron: Culinary Novices – here's another great example. Blue Apron caters to a niche of busy individuals who want to cook but lack time for meal planning. Their content includes easy recipes, cooking tips and meal prep guides, creating value for their specific audience. They provide step-by-step guides for cooking novices and emphasise the convenience of their meal kits.

And finally, Hootsuite. Hootsuite targets social media managers with content that delves deep into social media analytics, trends and tools. They create webinars, blog posts and case studies specifically tailored to the needs and challenges faced by social media professionals.

Metrics That Matter

In a later chapter we'll look at some different types of metrics that are worth measuring in more detail. For now, here's a summary of the metrics worth tracking when it comes to your niche content:

1. Audience Engagement

Track likes, comments, shares and overall interaction. High engagement indicates that your content is striking a chord with your audience. However, keep in mind that high engagement itself isn't the end goal. It's simply an indication that you're sharing content your market likes. Ultimately, your aim is for your content to lead your prospects through the buyer's journey, on to the sale and then recommending you to others.

2. *Conversion Rates*

Monitor how many leads from your niche audience convert into customers. High conversion rates mean your content is effectively persuading your specific market.

3. *Feedback and Surveys*

Actively seek feedback from your audience through surveys. Understand what they love, what they want more of and areas for improvement.

4. *Audience Growth in Your Niche*

Measure the growth of your audience within your niche. Are you attracting and retaining the right people?

The Ever-Evolving Niche

Over time, there will be many changes within your niche. If you don't keep up, you'll eventually be left behind.

Here are some ways you can stay on top of changes within your niche:

1. *Market Trends and Shifts*

Stay attuned to market trends and shifts in your niche. Flexibility in adapting your content strategy ensures relevance.

Regularly analyse industry reports and adjust your content calendar accordingly.

2. *Feedback Loop*

Establish a feedback loop with your audience. Regularly ask for feedback and adjust your content based on their evolving needs. Use a combination of social media polls, surveys and comments to gather insights.

3. *Competitor Analysis*

Keep an eye on your competitors within the niche. Understand what works for them, but more importantly, identify gaps you can fill. Conduct regular competitor analyses to stay ahead of industry changes.

Crafting Your Niche Content Strategy

Okay, content rockstar! Now it's time to take action. Following the guidelines from this chapter it's time for you to take some action and craft your niche content strategy.

Here's a summary of how to do that:

1. *Define Your Niche Clearly*

Precisely articulate who your niche is. The clearer your definition, the more effective your content strategy. Develop a detailed document outlining your niche, including demographics, psychographics and pain points.

2. Create Comprehensive Buyer Personas

Develop detailed buyer personas. The more you know about your audience, the better you can tailor your content. Conduct regular surveys and interviews to update and refine your buyer personas.

3. Diversify Your Content Types

Experiment with different content formats. A mix of blogs, videos and interactive content keeps your strategy dynamic. Test and analyse the performance of each content type to fine-tune your approach.

4. Consistency Is Key

Be consistent in your messaging, tone, and delivery. Consistency builds trust and reinforces your brand in the minds of your audience. Later in this book I'll walk you through how to create a content calendar. This helps make the whole process of consistently creating and sharing content easy-peasy!

Congratulations on mastering the art of nailing your niche through targeted content! Understanding and catering to your specific audience is the secret sauce that elevates your content marketing game.

As you move forward, the next chapter will delve into creating your fabulous ***Home Base***. This will be the heart and centre of your content platform.

PART 2:
HOME BASE

Welcome to **PART 2: HOME BASE**. Now, this is where we're diving deep into the heart of your content strategy. Think of it as your content's central hub – a place where a big chunk of your content will call home.

First things first, we'll uncover what exactly your Home Base is and why it's an absolute must-have in your toolkit.

Next up, we'll roll up our sleeves and get into the nitty-gritty of building a blog.

Now, what separates a great blog from the rest? We'll explore that too, along with what makes a blog post truly shine. And to top it off, we'll sprinkle in some valuable tips on getting your blog to strut its stuff in the search engines, especially our friend Google.

So, let's get ready to make your Home Base the powerhouse of your content strategy!

Chapter 4: Creating Your Home Base – The Ultimate Content Hub

Welcome, dear friend! Grab your coziest cup of tea because we're embarking on an exciting journey to create your very own Home Base – the cornerstone of your content marketing strategy.

Unveiling Your Home Base: The WordPress.org Blog

Let's start by shedding light on what this Home Base truly is. Quite simply – it's a blog. More specifically, a blog built using WordPress.org *(not WordPress.com)*.

This is more than a website. It's your digital sanctuary, the command centre of your online presence. This is where the magic happens and understanding its significance is key to your content marketing success.

A WordPress.org blog offers you unparalleled control and flexibility. Unlike other platforms, you're not bound by their rules and limitations. You're the master of your digital domain and that's powerful. With WordPress.org, you own your content, your design and your destiny.

While social platforms are great, and something you'll likely use too, the truth is that they can shut down or ban your account at any moment. What happens then?

If you've built your home base around your blog and followed these guidelines, you're all good. You won't have lost all content and contact with your audience.

The Essence of a Home Base

So, why is a Home Base a non-negotiable element in your content marketing toolkit?

Simply put, it's your digital anchor, your online headquarters. In the ever-changing landscape of the internet, having a place that's exclusively yours is priceless.

Imagine this: social media platforms are like trendy cafés where you meet your audience. But your Home Base? It's your own cozy corner café, where your audience knows they can always find you, enjoy your best brews and have meaningful conversations. No more worrying about algorithm changes or platform shutdowns. Your Home Base is your digital home and it's here to stay.

Crafting Your Blog: No Tech Panic Here!

Now, I understand that tech jargon can be intimidating, but building your blog doesn't require a tech genius. If the thought of plugins, widgets and coding sends shivers down your spine, don't worry. You can enlist the help of a professional to set up and manage the technical aspects.

Hiring a tech-savvy expert is like having a trusty handyman for your digital house. They'll ensure everything runs smoothly while you focus on creating amazing content. It's an investment in peace of mind. And quite frankly, your time is better spent doing what you do best.

Finding this tech-savvy guru to build your blog is as vital as choosing the right home builder for your dream house. Consider exploring freelance platforms like Upwork.com, Fiverr.com or Toptal.com where you can connect with experienced professionals who specialise in web development and WordPress.

Alternatively, ask for recommendations from fellow entrepreneurs or business groups. I love word-of-mouth referrals and find these often lead to fantastic collaborations.

Filling Your Home Base: Content is Key

Once your blog is up and running, it's time to give it life with your fantastic content. Your Home Base is your content's permanent residence – a place where your ideas, insights and stories find their forever home.

Now, if you're not sure about adding the content to your blog regularly, don't fret. Virtual Assistants *(VAs)* are brilliant at this. Give them some instructions and your content and they can help you organise and publish your content efficiently. This can be on your blog, but on your social media channels too. They can do all sorts of tasks to help you in your content marketing journey.

Think of them as your content co-pilots, working alongside you to make your Home Base thrive.

To find a good VA, again, the sites such as Upwork.com, Fiverr.com and Toptal.com are good places to find a VA or ask for referrals from your business network.

Crafting the Perfect Domain Name

Your blog's domain name is your online address. For example, www.TheContentClassroom.com. But it's more than a web address; it's your brand's digital identity.

Choosing the perfect domain name is like selecting the nameplate for your dream house – it should reflect your brand's personality, values and purpose.

Take your time with this decision because it's an integral part of your online identity. But don't procrastinate, okay?

A memorable domain name not only makes it easier for your audience to find you but also leaves a lasting impression.

GoDaddy.com is a good place to go to register your domain name.

Navigating the Hosting Maze

Now, let's demystify hosting. Think of it as renting a safe and reliable space on the internet where your blog and its content will live. It ensures your blog is accessible to anyone on the internet, anytime, without any technical hiccups.

Like choosing your physical home's location, selecting the right hosting provider is essential to ensure your Home Base operates seamlessly.

When scouting for a hosting provider, consider factors like speed, reliability, customer support, and scalability. Your hosting choice can significantly impact your website's performance, so it's worth doing your homework.

My personal preference is VentraIP.com.au, an Australian company. Another good hosting company with an excellent reputation is Bluehost.com.

Designing Your Blog: Creating a Welcoming Space

Designing your blog is akin to decorating your dream house. You want it to be inviting, easy to navigate and reflective of your brand's style and personality. Your blog's design sets the stage for your content and influences your audience's perception.

Whether you opt for a minimalist, sleek look or a colourful, vibrant aesthetic, your design should align with your brand's identity and appeal to your ideal audience. A well-thought-out layout enhances the user experience, making it enjoyable for your readers to explore your content.

Style Matters: Writing, Images and Presentation

Your Home Base is an extension of your brand and consistency is key. The style you choose for your writing, images and presentation should harmonise with your branding.

If you've followed along with our journey through Chapters 2 and 3, where we delved into discovering your brand story and targeting your content, you're well-equipped to make these choices.

Your writing style should reflect your brand's voice and values.

For example, are you informal and friendly or professional and authoritative?

Your choice should resonate with your target audience.

When it comes to images, select visuals that align with your brand's aesthetic. Consistency in your image style creates a cohesive visual identity that's instantly recognisable.

Presentation matters too. Your blog's layout, fonts, and colour schemes should be consistent with your brand guidelines. This uniformity creates a polished and professional appearance.

What Sets Your Blog Apart

What separates a great blog from the rest? It's not just the content – it's the infusion of your unique voice, perspective and personality into your content. Your Home Base should reflect you and your brand.

Your personal touch is what will make your Home Base an irresistible destination for your audience. Don't be afraid to inject your humour, quirks and authenticity into your content. It's what makes you stand out in a sea of digital voices.

Glimpse of Search Engine Visibility

While we won't dive too deep into this topic yet, understanding search engine visibility is crucial for your blog's success. In a later chapter, we'll explore SEO *(Search Engine Optimisation)* in greater detail, helping your content strut its stuff and rise to the top of search engine results.

By optimising your site and its content, you give your content its best chance of being found in the search engines when a potential customer searches on a term that your content can help them with.

When using WordPress for your Home Base, I highly recommend using the Yoast SEO plug-in *(for more details on this plug-in go to https://wordpress.org/plugins/wordpress-seo/)*. Although you can upgrade to the premium version for a fee, the free version of this plug-in is quite enough for most people. This will help you to optimise each of your WordPress site's pages and your blog content to help it get found in the search engines.

Before we wrap up, let's take a sneak peek at what's coming up in Chapter 5. We're going to explore the captivating world of content – blog posts, podcasts and videos... and so much more. Get ready for a journey into creating diverse content that engages and resonates with your audience.

So, Lovely, let's roll up our sleeves and create your Home Base – a place where your content thrives and your audience feels right at home. Until next time, sip your tea, embrace your creativity and I'll see you in Chapter 5!

PART 3:
CONTENT

In this section, we'll explore different types of content, how to create it and how to leverage it in your business.

Remember, you don't have to use every content type right away. You can start with one form of content and get comfortable with it. Once you've mastered that or found someone proficient to help, you can gradually add more content types to your strategy.

Don't let yourself feel overwhelmed; there's no rush to do everything at once.

Perfection isn't the goal either. Sometimes, "good enough" is perfectly fine for now. The key is to make it "good enough" at this stage and you'll naturally improve as you gain experience.

It's important to know that many successful content creators began with content that was okay or even not-so-great and improved over time *(myself included)*.

So, embrace the learning journey and you'll see progress along the way. Let's dig in, shall we?

Chapter 5: Mastering the Content Mix: Blogs, Podcasts, and Videos

Exploring the Various Content Formats and Finding the Right Mix for Your Business and Audience

Hello, fabulous reader! Welcome to Chapter 5 of our content marketing journey. Today, we're diving into the exciting world of content formats. From the timeless allure of blogs to the captivating power of podcasts and the visual feast of videos, we're going to unravel the intricacies of each format.

So, grab your notepad, maybe a second cup of coffee, and let's explore how to master the art of the content mix.

The Content Landscape: A Symphony of Formats

The Rise of Diverse Content

Your audience is diverse in preferences and tastes, engaging with your brand through various channels. That's the beauty of a well-curated content mix. In a world saturated with information, offering a variety of content formats ensures you meet your audience where they are.

Imagine your brand as the conductor, orchestrating a masterpiece that captivates and engages your audience across various channels.

The Symphony of Audience Diversity

A Tapestry of Tastes

Your audience is a rich tapestry of individuals with unique preferences, tastes and habits. Like in a symphony where different instruments contribute to the overall composition, your audience's unique preferences contribute to the vibrancy of your content landscape.

Engagement Across Channels

It's important to understand that some members of your audience may prefer taking in your information through thoughtful blog posts, savouring each word, while others may be drawn to the dynamic energy of podcasts, listening on the go. Then there are those who prefer more visual forms of learning who resonate better with videos.

Meeting Your Audience Where They Are

In a world where attention is a precious commodity and online spaces are vast, meeting your audience where they are becomes essential.

Understanding the range of preferences of your audience is like fine-tuning your instruments before a performance – it ensures that every note, every piece of content, resonates in harmony with their expectations.

The Importance Of Understanding Your Audience

1. Building Connection

Understanding your audience is the foundation of building a meaningful connection. It's about speaking their language, addressing their pain points and celebrating their victories. Genuinely. When you tailor your content to their preferences, you show that you not only value their time but also respect their individuality.

2. Enhancing Relevance

In the content landscape, relevance is the key to capturing attention. By understanding the content formats your audience prefers, you're not just delivering information; you're creating an experience that aligns with their expectations. This relevance is the bridge that connects your brand to their daily lives.

3. Driving Engagement

Different segments of your audience engage with content in distinct ways. Some may thrive on in-depth blog posts that offer deep insights, while others may engage more readily with the personal touch of a podcast. By offering a variety of content formats, you maximise the opportunities for engagement, ensuring that each member of your audience finds something that resonates.

Someone doesn't have time *(or patience)* to read a book? No problem. They may prefer to watch videos. Or listen to audio.

4. Tailoring Content Delivery

Not only is the type of content important, but the delivery platforms also play a crucial role. Are your target customers more likely to be found scrolling through Instagram, tuning in to Spotify or reading industry blogs? By understanding the platforms your audience is more likely to hang out on, you can strategically place your content where it's most likely to be discovered.

In "Nailing Your Niche," we explored the power of niche content. Understanding your audience's preferences is the first step in tailoring niche content that speaks directly to their interests and needs. The better you know your audience, the more precise and impactful your niche content can be.

Crafting Your Content Symphony

1. Conducting Audience Surveys

Engage with your audience directly through surveys to gain insights into their content preferences. Ask questions about the types of content they enjoy, the platforms they frequent and the topics that resonate with them.

2. Analysing Analytics Data

Leverage the analytics data from your website, social media and other platforms. Understand which types of content receive the most engagement, shares and comments. Analysing this data provides valuable clues about your audience's content consumption habits.

3. Social Media Listening

Monitor social media conversations related to your industry and brand. Social media platforms are not only channels for content distribution but also hubs of discussions. By actively listening to your audience on these platforms, you can gauge their sentiments, preferences and trending topics.

4. A/B Testing Content Formats

Experiment with different content formats and measure the audience response. A/B testing allows you to compare the performance of, for example, blog posts against podcasts or videos.

Through iterative testing, you can refine your content strategy based on what resonates most with your audience.

5. Aligning with Business Goals

Understanding your audience goes hand in hand with aligning your content strategy with your business goals. If your goal is lead generation, knowing the types of content that convert leads is essential. Similarly, if brand awareness is a priority, tailoring content for wider reach becomes crucial.

The Ever-Evolving Symphony

Remember, the content landscape and audience preferences are not static. They evolve over time, influenced by industry trends, technological advancements and shifting consumer behaviours. As a content conductor, stay attuned to these changes, continuously refining your content mix to maintain a harmonious connection with your audience.

Next, let's have a look at some of the main types of content in this symphony of formats.

1. Blogs: The Timeless Craft of Written Word

The Art of Blogging

Blogs are the heartbeat of content marketing, and for good reason. They provide a platform for in-depth exploration, thought leadership and the evergreen charm of the written word. Whether you're a budding entrepreneur or a seasoned business owner, mastering the art of blogging is like having a secret weapon in your marketing arsenal.

And as we discussed in the previous chapter, blogs are the perfect 'Home Base' for your content.

Here are some tips on how to create blog posts that keep your audience coming back for more... and taking action to move through their customer journey with you:

Crafting Compelling Blogs
1. Headlines that Hook
    o The first impression matters. Craft headlines that grab attention and spark curiosity.
    o *Example: "Unleashing the Power of [Your Product] - A Comprehensive Guide"*

2. Structured for Skim-ability
   o Break down content into digestible sections with subheadings, bullet points and visuals.
   o *Example: Use infographics or images to illustrate key points.*

3. SEO Magic
   o Infuse relevant keywords naturally to enhance search engine visibility.
   o *Example: If you're a fitness coach, incorporate terms like "healthy lifestyle" and "fitness tips."*

4. Engaging Opening and Closing
   o Hook readers from the start and leave them with a compelling call to action.
   o *Example: Begin with a relatable scenario and conclude with an invitation to share their thoughts in the comments or to opt-in for your free gift.*

The Power of Blogs in Numbers

Here's are some stats to help demonstrate the power of blogs:

SEO Boost:
  Websites with blogs have 434% more indexed pages within the search engines, leading to higher visibility. Which means... more people find your website.

Lead Generation:
  Businesses that prioritise blogging experience 67% more leads than those that don't.

Establishing Authority:
  Regular blogging helps businesses build authority in their industry.

2. Podcasts: Voices in the Airwaves

The Rise of Audio Content
  In a world where multitasking is the norm, podcasts have become a go-to source of information and entertainment. The intimacy of voice creates a unique connection, allowing your audience to absorb content while on the go.

Crafting Compelling Podcasts
  1. Captivating Introductions

- o Start with a hook that piques curiosity and sets the tone for the episode.
- o *Example: "Welcome to [Podcast Name], where we unravel the secrets of [Industry] success!"*

2. Guests and Collaborations
   - o Bring in experts, influencers or complementary businesses to add variety and expertise.
   - o *Example: Invite a thought leader for a deep dive into a relevant industry topic.*

3. Narrative Flow
   - o Plan episodes with a clear structure – introduction, main content and a memorable conclusion.
   - o *Example: Create segments or recurring features to add consistency.*

4. Promotion Through Repurposing
   - o Transcribe episodes into blog posts, share key insights on social media and create video snippets.
   - o *Example: Share a quote or key takeaway from the episode as a teaser on Instagram.*

The Power of Podcasts in Numbers

Audience Growth:
In 2021, there were over 850,000 active podcasts and more than 30 million podcast episodes. This has continued to grow since then.

Brand Loyalty:
80% of podcast listeners hear all or most of the episodes of their favourite shows.

Advertising Impact:
Podcast advertising spending globally was predicted to reach over $3.4 billion by the end of 2023 and projected to reach US$5.26 billion by 2028.

3. Videos: A Visual Symphony

The Visual Powerhouse
Videos are the rockstars of content. They combine the potency of visuals, audio and storytelling to deliver a memorable and engaging experience. In the era of short attention spans, videos are your ticket to grabbing eyeballs and holding onto them.

Crafting Compelling Videos
    1. Storytelling through Visuals

- o Plan videos with a narrative arc. Use visuals to enhance the story and evoke emotions.
- o *Example: Create a video showcasing the journey of a customer using your product.*

2. Diversify Video Types
    - o Experiment with different video formats – tutorials, behind-the-scenes, testimonials and more.
    - o *Example: Host a live Q&A session or a product launch event on video.*

3. Optimised for Social Media
    - o Tailor videos for each platform, considering aspect ratios, captions and engagement features.
    - o *Example: Create short, engaging snippets for Instagram and longer-form content for YouTube.*

4. Call to Action Within Videos
    - o Direct viewers on the next steps – whether it's visiting your website, subscribing or making a purchase.
    - o *Example: End the video with a clear call to action, such as subscribing to your channel or exploring your products.*

The Power of Videos in Numbers

Consumption Trends:
78% of people watch online videos every week and 55% view online videos every day.

Engagement Boost:
Social media videos generate 12 times more shares than text and images combined.

Conversion Impact:
Including a video on a landing page can increase conversion rates by 80%.

Finding Your Content Mix Symphony

The Harmonious Blend
Creating a content mix is not about choosing one format over another – it's about orchestrating a harmonious blend that resonates with your audience.

As we progress through this book, we'll continue to explore how to find the right mix for your business.

Embracing the Symphony
Congratulations! You've now embarked on the journey of mastering the content mix. Whether it's the timeless elegance of blogs, the intimate connection of podcasts or the visual feast of

videos, each format contributes to the symphony of your content strategy.

In the next chapter, we'll delve into the world of storytelling. Until then, may your content mix resonate with your audience like a perfectly tuned orchestra!

Chapter 6: Creating Captivating Content: The Art of Storytelling

Techniques to Weave Compelling Stories that Engage and Connect with Your Audience

Hello, Gorgeous! Welcome back... and prepare yourself for a deep dive into the enchanting realm of storytelling!

In this chapter, we'll not only explore the magic of storytelling but uncover the secrets to creating narratives that capture attention and forge lasting connections.

So, grab your favourite mug of inspiration and let's embark on this journey where words become spells.

The Power of Storytelling

Unleashing the Magic
Picture this: A room filled with people, all eyes on a storyteller who spins a tale that transports everyone to a different world.

That's the power of storytelling.

It's not just a tool; it's a form of magic that can transform ordinary content into an extraordinary experience. This magic, my friend, is what forges an emotional bond between you and your audience.

Connecting Through Narratives

Why do we love stories?

Because they connect us. They transport us to different worlds, evoke emotions and make us feel part of something bigger. Your content has the same potential – to be a bridge that connects your audience to your brand on a profound level.

Let's unravel the threads of this magical tapestry.

Understanding the Anatomy of a Great Story

The Hero's Journey

Every great story follows a pattern – the Hero's Journey. Whether it's Harry Potter battling dark forces or a small business owner overcoming challenges, the stages are the same.

Understanding this structure helps you craft narratives that resonate. It's like having a roadmap for creating stories that captivate.

1. **The Call to Adventure**
   o Introduce a challenge or opportunity that beckons the hero *(your audience)*.
   o Example: Present a scenario that reflects a common challenge your audience faces.
2. **Meeting the Mentor**
   o Provide guidance or a solution, positioning your brand as the mentor aiding the hero.
   o Example: Share a success story of someone who overcame a similar challenge with your product/service.
3. **Crossing the Threshold**
   o The hero commits to the journey, mirroring your audience's decision to engage with your content.
   o Example: Illustrate the moment your audience decides to explore your content further.
4. **Challenges and Temptations**
   o The hero faces obstacles – reflecting the struggles and decisions your audience encounters.
   o Example: Highlight common pitfalls and challenges your audience might encounter.

5. **Atonement and Transformation**
   - The hero emerges transformed, just as your audience should after engaging with your content.
   - Example: Showcase the positive outcomes or transformations your audience can achieve.

Emotional Resonance

The heart of storytelling lies in emotion. Craft stories that tap into a range of feelings – joy, empathy, excitement or even a touch of nostalgia. Emotional resonance ensures your stories linger in the minds and hearts of your audience.

Techniques for Compelling Storytelling

1. Know Your Audience's Story

Before you tell your story, know theirs. Understand their challenges, dreams and aspirations. Your story should align with and speak to their narrative.

- **Dig Deep into Audience Insights**
  - Use analytics, surveys and social media listening to understand your audience's preferences and pain points.
  - Example: Conduct a survey to gather insights into your

audience's challenges and aspirations.

- **Craft Personas that Resonate**
  - o Develop detailed buyer personas that represent the real struggles and aspirations of your audience.
  - o Example: Create fictional characters that embody the characteristics of your target audience.

2. Start with a Bang

Capture attention from the outset. Whether it's an intriguing question, a startling fact or a relatable scenario, make the opening impossible to ignore.

- **Craft Attention-Grabbing Openers**
  - o Experiment with different opening techniques, such as posing a thought-provoking question or sharing a surprising statistic.
  - o Example: Start with a relatable scenario that immediately draws readers in.
- **Use Power Words**
  - o Incorporate strong and evocative words that elicit emotions and curiosity.
  - o Example: Use words like "Discover," "Uncover," or

"Revolutionise" to convey a sense of excitement... but only if these words are accurate, of course.

3. *Show, Don't Just Tell*

Paint vivid pictures with your words. Instead of stating facts, immerse your audience in experiences. Engage their senses and let them feel the story.

- **Create Vivid Imagery**
  - ○ Use descriptive language that paints a clear picture. Appeal to the senses to make the story more immersive.
  - ○ Example: Instead of saying "Our product is high-quality," describe its texture, scent or visual appeal.
- **Use Analogies and Metaphors**
  - ○ Analogies and metaphors can simplify complex concepts and make the narrative more relatable.
  - ○ Example: Compare a challenging business situation to navigating a turbulent sea, creating a visual metaphor.

4. *Create Relatable Characters*

Your audience is the hero. Introduce relatable characters – people who faced challenges similar to theirs and emerged victorious.

- **Share Customer Success Stories**
  - o Feature real stories of customers who achieved success with your product or service.
  - o Example: Showcase a customer's journey, detailing the challenges they faced and how your solution made a difference.
- **Highlight Employee Stories**
  - o Humanise your brand by sharing stories of employees who contribute to the company's mission.
  - o Example: Introduce team members, their roles and their passion for the company's mission.

5. Build Tension and Release

Keep your audience on the edge of their seats. Introduce challenges, create anticipation and then provide a resolution. It's the ebb and flow that keeps people engaged.

- **Introduce Plot Twists**
  - o Surprise your audience with unexpected turns in the story to maintain intrigue.
  - o Example: Share a turning point in your company's history that led to a significant breakthrough.

- **Use Cliffhangers**
  - End sections of your content with suspenseful moments that encourage readers to continue.
  - Example: Tease upcoming content or developments in your brand's journey.

6. *Use Conversational Language*

Imagine you're having a chat with a friend. Your tone should be conversational, making your audience feel like you're speaking directly to them.

- **Avoid Jargon**
  - Speak in a language your audience understands. Avoid industry jargon that might alienate them.
  - Example: Explain complex concepts using simple, everyday language.
- **Ask Rhetorical Questions**
  - Engage your audience by posing rhetorical questions that invite them to reflect on the story.
  - Example: "Have you ever faced a situation where..."

7. Incorporate Humour and Wit

Humour is a universal language. A well-timed joke or a playful anecdote humanises your brand and makes your content memorable.

But there are a few things to keep in mind when using humour:

- **Know Your Audience's Humour Preferences**
  - o Tailor humour to match your audience's preferences. Consider cultural nuances and sensitivities too.
  - o Example: Share light-hearted anecdotes related to your brand's journey or industry trends.
- **Use Humorous Anecdotes**
  - o Share amusing stories or experiences related to your brand or team.
  - o Example: Narrate a funny incident from your company's history that reflects your brand's personality. Or perhaps something that you did or said personally, to share some humour.

8. Inject Personal Experiences

Share your journey. Be vulnerable. Your personal experiences add authenticity and connect you with your audience on a deeper level.

- **Share Milestones and Challenges**
  - o Open up about the challenges your brand faced and celebrate milestones.
  - o Example: Reflect on a pivotal moment in your entrepreneurial journey and the lessons learned.
- **Showcase Behind-the-Scenes Moments**
  - o Provide a glimpse into the daily life of your business. Humanise your brand by showcasing real moments.
  - o Example: Share photos or anecdotes from team events or the creative process behind a product.

9. Create a Compelling Arc

Craft a narrative arc that takes your audience on a journey. From introduction to climax to resolution, each part should be purposeful.

- **Structure Your Storytelling**
  - o Outline your story with a clear beginning, middle and end. Ensure each section contributes to the overall narrative.

- Example: Map out the key points of your brand's story, ensuring a logical and engaging flow.
- **Emphasise Turning Points**
  - Identify key turning points in your brand's journey and highlight them for added impact.
  - Example: Narrate a pivotal decision or event that shaped your brand's direction.

10. End with a Call to Action

Every story should guide your audience towards action. Whether it's sharing the story, engaging with your brand or making a purchase, end with a clear call to action *(CTA)*.

- **Align CTA with Story Theme**
  - Ensure your call to action resonates with the theme of your story. It should feel like a natural next step.
  - Example: If your story is about overcoming challenges, the call to action could encourage readers to share their own triumphs.
- **Create Urgency**
  - Use language that conveys a sense of urgency. Encourage immediate action related to the story. *(But make sure the urgency is genuine. Don't say*

> *something won't be available after tomorrow, for example, if it will be.)*
>
> o Example: "Join us on this journey today – don't miss out on the next chapter of our story!"

Examples of Compelling Storytelling

1. Nike's "Just Do It" Campaign

- The hero: Anyone with a dream. The mentor: Nike. The call to adventure: Pursue your dreams. Emotional resonance: Empowerment and determination.
- *Example: Nike's campaign featured stories of individuals overcoming obstacles to achieve their goals. The relatable narratives resonated globally, positioning Nike as a brand that champions personal victories.*

2. Coca-Cola's "Share a Coke" Campaign

- The hero: Individuals craving connection. The mentor: Coca-Cola. The call to adventure: Share a Coke with a loved one. Emotional resonance: Joy, nostalgia and shared moments.
- *Example: Coca-Cola's campaign personalised their product by featuring common names on bottles, encouraging people to share a Coke with friends and*

family. The campaign created a sense of connection and joy.

3. Airbnb's "Belong Anywhere" Campaign

- The hero: Travelers seeking unique experiences. The mentor: Airbnb. The call to adventure: Experience the world as a local. Emotional resonance: Freedom, exploration and cultural connection.
- *Example: Airbnb's campaign told stories of travellers finding unique and personalised accommodations. By emphasising the idea of "belonging anywhere," the brand connected emotionally with a diverse audience.*

Measuring the Impact of Your Stories

1. Engagement Metrics

- Track likes, comments and shares. High engagement indicates your story struck a chord.
- *Example: Monitor social media metrics and website analytics to gauge how well your audience responded to the story. A spike in engagement often signifies resonance.*

2. Brand Sentiment

- Monitor how your audience perceives your brand after storytelling efforts.

Positive sentiment is a testament to effective storytelling.

- *Example: Conduct surveys to measure changes in brand sentiment before and after storytelling campaigns. Analyse feedback to identify areas of improvement.*

3. Conversion Rates

- Analyse how storytelling impacts conversion rates. Compelling stories should guide your audience towards action.
- *Example: Compare conversion rates before and after launching a storytelling campaign. Identify the specific actions taken by those who engaged with the story.*

Crafting Your Storytelling Strategy

1. Align Stories with Brand Values

- Ensure your stories align with your brand's core values. Consistency builds trust.
- *Example: If sustainability is a core value, ensure that your stories highlight environmentally friendly practices and initiatives.*

2. Test and Iterate

- Experiment with different storytelling approaches. Analyse what resonates best with your audience and refine your strategy accordingly.

- *Example: Test two different story formats or themes to understand which ones generate the most engagement. (A/B testing.) Use insights to optimise future storytelling efforts.*

3. *Create a Story Bank*

- Build a repository of stories. This ensures a steady supply for various marketing channels and occasions.

- *Example: Develop a content calendar that includes a variety of stories, ensuring a consistent and diverse narrative. Update the story bank regularly.*

4. *Incorporate User-Generated Stories*

- Encourage your audience to share their stories. User-generated content adds authenticity and diversity to your narrative.

- *Example: Launch a social media campaign inviting followers to share their experiences with your brand. Feature the most compelling user stories on your website and marketing materials.*

Embrace the Magic of Storytelling

Congratulations! You've now unlocked the secrets of creating captivating content through the art of storytelling. As you weave narratives that resonate, remember that every story is a brushstroke on the canvas of your brand.

In the next chapter, we'll explore the enchanting realm of Visual Storytelling: Graphics, Images and Brand Aesthetics. Get ready to discover how visual elements can be harnessed to elevate your content and strengthen your brand identity.

Until then, keep weaving those magical tales, and may your words continue to cast spells of connection and engagement!

Chapter 7: Visual Storytelling: Graphics, Images and Brand Aesthetics

Using Visual Elements to Enhance Your Content and Reinforce Your Brand Identity

Hey there, Lovely. It's so good to have you back! As I write this chapter, I'm sitting cozily in my office with two sleepy kitties dreaming peacefully either side of my feet. Honestly, I feel so grateful to be able to call this my 'work' and I truly hope you're getting a lot out of this book so far.

If you're not already comfortable, quickly do what you need to so that you are, grab your favourite drink, a notebook and pen, and let's dive into the colourful world of visual storytelling. You're about to discover how visuals can transform your content from good to unforgettable. So, let's get started!

Why Visuals Matter in Content Marketing

Did you know...

...articles with images get 94% more views than those without? That's not a little bump; it's a content game-changer!

Visuals do more than catch the eye; they evoke emotions and help your content stick in your audience's memory.

When people hear information, they remember only 10% of it three days later. But if a relevant image is paired with that same information, retention jumps to 65%.

Plus, for Twitter – or X – users, Tweets with images receive 150% more retweets than tweets without images.

As an example, let's say you're writing about home office organisation. A paragraph describing a tidy, well-lit space is fine, but add a picture showing a sun-drenched desk with neatly arranged plants and stationery and BOOM! Your readers are not just reading; they're experiencing.

The Psychology Behind Visual Content

We, as humans, are wired to process and respond to visuals. It's not merely about what we see... it's about what we feel when we see it.

Time and time again colours have been proven to evoke certain emotions. For example:

- **Blue:** Trust and calmness. Perfect for consultants and coaches.
- **Red:** Excitement and urgency. Great for calls to action.
- **Green:** Growth and health. Ideal for wellness brands.

These are just 3 examples of how colours are often perceived and the emotions they invoke. A quick search on Google.com will bring up many sites that can give you more details on these colour/emotion links if you're interested in knowing more.

Similarly, shapes and lines can evoke certain emotions too. For example:

- **Circles:** Community and unity.
- **Squares:** Stability and professionalism.
- **Lines:** Direction and movement.

Visual Storytelling in Action:

A financial advisor might use images of open skies and serene landscapes to convey a sense of freedom and peace that comes with financial security.

Whereas wellness coaches often use greens or bright, vibrant fruits and vegetables to help represent health, along with images of the outdoors.

Crafting Your Visual Brand Identity

Your visual brand identity is your brand's visual voice. It will help to set you apart in a noisy online world.

Steps to Create Your Visual Identity:
So, how do you go about creating your visual identity?

1. **Define Your Brand Personality:** Are you bold and vibrant or subtle and sophisticated?

2. **Choose Your Colour Palette:** Stick to a consistent set of colours that reflect your brand's personality.

3. **Select Your Typography:** Your fonts should match the tone of your brand. A playful font is not usually going to work well for a law firm aiming for a serious, professional image.

4. **Develop a Style for Your Images:** Decide on a specific style for your images that reflects your brand. This could be candid and natural, polished and professional or perhaps quirky and fun.

Once you've created your visual identity, make sure that everyone in your team is aware of this, if you have staff or team members.

Then make sure you stick with this visual branding within all your content.

The Role of Graphics and Images in Telling Your Brand's Story

Every visual you share tells a part of your brand's story. Think of your visuals as chapters of a book – each one contributes to the overall narrative.

Visual Consistency:
- **Brand Recognition:** Consistent use of colours, fonts and imagery makes your brand instantly recognisable. Think of Coca-Cola – their red and white colour scheme is iconic.
- **Brand Cohesion:** Across all platforms, your visuals should tell a cohesive story. If your Instagram is modern and minimalistic, your website should follow suit.

Leveraging Different Types of Visuals:
It's also good to include different types of visuals, such as:
- **Photographs:** Show real-life glimpses of your brand.
- **Graphics and Illustrations:** Great for explaining concepts and adding a creative touch.
- **Videos:** Ideal for storytelling and engaging content.

For example, a yoga instructor could use a mix of serene studio photos, calming graphics of nature and video snippets of classes to convey a sense of peace and community.

Best Practices for Using Visuals in Your Content

Here are some tips on best practices when it comes to your visual content:

1. **Keep It High Quality:** Always use high-resolution images. Blurry or pixelated images can make your brand look unprofessional. *(You can use a tool such as TinyPNG.com to create smaller sized files for high resolution images. This will help them load quicker on your website, without losing the quality.)*

2. **Stay Authentic:** Use images that truly represent your services. Your audience can spot inauthenticity from a mile away.

3. **Diversity and Inclusion:** Show a range of people in your visuals, where possible.

Tools and Resources for Creating Stunning Visuals

- **Canva.com:** Perfect for non-designers. It's packed with templates for social media graphics, presentations, and more.

- **Unsplash.com and Pexels.com:** For high-quality, free stock photos that don't look 'stocky'.
- **TinyPNG.com:** To create smaller sized images from your high-resolution images, without compromising on the quality.

Incorporating Visuals into Different Types of Content

- **Blog Posts:** Break up your text with relevant images, infographics or videos. They make your post more readable and engaging.
- **Social Media:** Tailor your visuals for each platform. Instagram loves aesthetically pleasing images, while LinkedIn prefers more professional content.
- **Text Documents:** Documents that are text only can be heavy on the eye. Sometimes you can include images to help break up the text. Other times you can use colour and different fonts to highlight certain areas. In books where it's preferred that you don't include images for formatting or technical purposes, such as this book, make sure you use lots of formatting such as sub-headings, bullet points and bold fonts.

Again, this helps to break up the text and make it easier to read.

Measuring the Success of Your Visual Content

It's not just about creating beautiful visuals; it's about creating visuals that work. Track the performance of your visuals through engagement rates *(how many people engage with your content)*, click-through rates *(also known as CTR – how many people follow through on your call to action)* and conversion rates *(how many people convert into leads, customers or repeat customers)*.

Common Mistakes to Avoid in Visual Storytelling

Two of the biggest mistakes I see over and over again in visual storytelling are:

1. **Ignoring Your Brand Voice:** Every visual should feel as if it's a part of your brand family.
2. **Following Every Trend:** It's okay to be inspired by trends, but don't lose your brand's unique voice in the process.

Wrapping Up and Looking Ahead

Your visuals are powerful storytellers. They can turn your brand's message into an experience that resonates with your audience. So, take the time to craft visuals that truly reflect your brand's heart and soul.

At the time of writing this book I'm also in the process of refining my brand. This is a HUGE job. I didn't realise just how much content I've created over the years! So, it's a work in progress. As a famous saying goes, it won't happen overnight, but it will happen. ;-)

Your Next Step: Review your current visual assets. Do they align with your brand's voice and message? If not, it's time for a visual brand refresh!

And hey, before you go, let's sneak a peek at what's coming up next. In the next chapter, we're going to have a chat about Lead Magnets. *(What the...?)* Don't worry if you don't know what these are. All will be revealed!

PART 4:
LEAD MAGNET

Welcome to **PART 4: LEAD MAGNET**, your gateway to unlocking the art of lead generation and nurturing. In this section, we'll embark on a journey that explores the creation and deployment of your lead magnet, a potent tool in your content marketing arsenal.

We'll start by unravelling the concept of a lead magnet – what it is and why it's a game-changer. Think of it as the irresistible offering you provide to potential customers in exchange for their precious contact information. This initial connection sets the stage for deeper engagement and relationship-building.

We'll delve into what makes a lead magnet compelling and why building and nurturing your email list is paramount in content marketing. Plus, you'll understand the significance of growing your list and how it becomes your direct line of communication with your audience.

Get ready to dive into the world of lead magnets and email marketing mastery. It's time to turn prospects into devoted customers and elevate your content marketing game.

Chapter 8: Unveiling The Power Of Lead Magnets

Welcome to Chapter 8, where we're about to dive into the enchanting world of lead magnets – one of the most dynamic and game-changing tools in your content marketing arsenal. So, my beautiful friend, make sure you're comfy and have your favourite drink with you... maybe even your trusty pen and notebook because you're going to want to capture every golden nugget of wisdom we're about to uncover.

The Magic of Lead Magnets:

Let's kick off with the most fundamental question: What exactly is a lead magnet and why is it so essential?

Imagine it as a magnetic force, drawing potential customers – leads – toward your business. It's a valuable offering you extend to them in exchange for their precious contact details, such as their name and email address.

This initial connection is the crucial first step in building lasting relationships through email – an absolute cornerstone of your content marketing journey.

But what makes a lead magnet truly magical?

It's the promise of solving a problem or fulfilling a need that your audience deeply cares about.

The Spectrum of Irresistible Gifts:

Now, let's talk about the spectrum of irresistible gifts you can offer as lead magnets. The options are boundless, limited only by your creativity. Think webinars, videos, ebooks, templates, checklists, resource guides – anything that holds high perceived value for your prospects and aligns with their desires.

Now, let's dive deep into the world of crafting lead magnets that your audience won't be able to resist. This is where your creativity can truly shine, and the possibilities are only limited by your imagination.

1. Audience-Centric Brainstorming: Start by putting yourself in your audience's shoes.

- *What are their pain points, challenges, and desires?*
- *What valuable information or solutions can you offer that will address these issues?*

Remember, your lead magnet should provide immediate value and demonstrate your expertise.

Brainstorm ideas that align with your niche and your audience's specific needs.

2. High-Value Content: Your lead magnet should offer something of genuine value. It could be a comprehensive guide, a step-by-step tutorial, a checklist, a resource list or even access to an exclusive webinar. Ensure that the content provides actionable insights or solves a real problem your audience faces. And don't be afraid to give away your valuable content. The more you give, the more you'll receive.

3. Solving a Problem: People are drawn to lead magnets that promise to solve a pressing problem. Identify a common challenge within your niche and create a lead magnet that offers a practical solution. Use your lead magnet as a teaser of the valuable solutions you provide through your products or services.

4. Clear and Compelling Titles: Your lead magnet's title should grab your audience's attention and clearly communicate its value. Craft a title that conveys the benefit of downloading the lead magnet. For example, ***"Unlock the Secrets to Effortless Productivity"*** is more captivating than a vague title along the lines of ***"Productivity Tips."***

5. Visually Appealing Design: Presentation matters. Ensure your lead magnet looks professional and visually appealing. If it's an ebook or PDF guide, invest in a well-designed cover and layout. Visual elements can significantly enhance the perceived value of your lead magnet.

6. Bite-Sized and Actionable: Consider breaking down complex topics into easily digestible, actionable steps. People appreciate lead magnets that don't overwhelm them but instead guide them towards achieving a specific outcome. Make it easy for your audience to implement your advice.

7. Test and Refine: Don't be afraid to experiment with different lead magnet formats and topics. Test various options to see what resonates best with your audience. Collect feedback and track the performance of your lead magnets to make continuous improvements.

8. Packaging and Delivery: Once you've created your lead magnet, pay attention to how you package and deliver it. Ensure the download process is smooth and user-friendly. Create a compelling landing page that highlights the benefits of your lead magnet and includes an easy opt-in form.

By following these practical tips and considering the unique needs of your audience, you'll be well on your way to creating lead magnets that not only attract but genuinely captivate your prospects.

Remember, your goal is to provide immediate value and establish trust, setting the stage for long-lasting relationships with your audience.

The Anatomy of an Exceptional Lead Magnet:

So, what transforms a good lead magnet into a truly exceptional one?

The answer lies in its ability to go beyond surface-level solutions and genuinely impact your audience's lives. Let's delve into strategies that will not only educate but also create transformational experiences for those who engage with your lead magnet.

1. Identify Deep Pain Points: Exceptional lead magnets address profound pain points and challenges your audience faces. To achieve this, you must have a deep understanding of your target audience's struggles. Dive into surveys, social media conversations and direct interactions to uncover the issues that keep them awake at night. Your lead magnet should promise relief from these pressing concerns.

2. The Power of Empathy: Demonstrating empathy is key to creating transformational lead magnets. Your audience should feel understood and supported from the moment they encounter your offer. Craft your messaging in a way that shows you're not just offering a solution but also genuinely care about their well-being.

3. Storytelling that Resonates: Stories have the power to connect on an emotional level. Weave relatable stories into your lead magnet that mirror the experiences of your audience. Narratives create a sense of belonging and validation, making your lead magnet more compelling and relatable.

4. Actionable Insights: Lead magnets that educate and transform provide actionable insights that your audience can implement immediately. Offer step-by-step guides, templates or frameworks that guide them towards solving their problem. People appreciate tangible takeaways that lead to real progress.

5. Visual Appeal: Visual elements enhance the effectiveness of your lead magnet. Use engaging graphics, charts and images to break down complex concepts or illustrate key points. Visuals not only make your lead magnet more digestible but also reinforce the value you're providing.

6. Clear Transformational Path: Outline a clear path to transformation within your lead magnet. Explain how engaging with your content will lead to positive changes in their lives. People are more likely to take action when they see a well-defined journey towards improvement.

7. Leverage the Psychology of Persuasion: Persuasion psychology plays a significant role in crafting exceptional lead magnets. Incorporate principles like social proof, scarcity and reciprocity to boost engagement and conversions. Highlight success stories, testimonials or limited time offers to persuade your audience to take action.

8. Offer Personalisation: Tailor your lead magnet to the specific needs and preferences of your audience segments. Personalisation creates a stronger connection and increases the perceived value of your offer. Consider offering different versions of your lead magnet to cater to diverse audience segments.

By implementing these strategies, you'll be well on your way to crafting lead magnets that not only educate but also inspire transformation in the lives of your audience. Remember, the goal is to provide solutions that resonate deeply, building trust and positioning your brand as a valuable resource on their journey to improvement.

Why Your Email List Matters in Your Content Marketing Strategy:

Now that you've perfected the art of crafting enticing lead magnets, let's explore the profound significance of building and nurturing your email list, unravelling how it can become your secret weapon in the realm of content marketing.

1. The Power of Direct Connection: Imagine having an exclusive, direct line to your audience, where you can effortlessly share your content and messages without any intermediaries. Picture this as your secret sauce – your email list offers precisely that. It establishes a direct connection to your subscribers, enabling you to seamlessly disseminate your content, free from external distractions or algorithms.

2. Stellar Conversion Rates for Content: Email marketing consistently boasts some of the highest conversion rates when it comes to promoting content in the digital marketing landscape. So, it's a powerhouse for driving audience engagement with your content.

3. Tailored Engagement for Your Content:
Email's unique power lies in personalisation. You have the ability to craft content and offers tailored precisely to your subscribers' preferences and behaviours. Segmenting your list allows you to send customised content to various audience segments, boosting the relevance of your messages and deepening engagement with your content. Personalisation ultimately leads to higher open and click-through rates, translating into more conversions.

4. Cultivating Trust Through Content:
Building trust is a cornerstone of converting subscribers into dedicated consumers of your content. Through consistent and valuable email communication, you nurture trust with your audience concerning the content you provide. As your subscribers receive valuable insights, solutions to their content-related challenges and helpful resources, they begin to trust your expertise and authority in your niche. Trust is the linchpin for converting subscribers into avid readers, viewers, customers and advocates of your products and services.

5. Ownership and Control for Content:
Unlike social media platforms or other third-party channels, your email list is an asset that you own and manage. It serves as a valuable

resource for content distribution, giving you full control. You won't be subject to the whims of external platforms' policies or algorithms, ensuring that your list remains accessible and valuable, regardless of external changes or challenges.

6. Sustained Engagement with Your Content: Email marketing excels at maintaining ongoing engagement with your audience and your content. By consistently delivering valuable content, insights and offers, you can ensure your brand and content stay top of mind. Subscribers who regularly interact with your content are more likely to become loyal readers, viewers and customers, bolstering your content's overall success.

7. Cost-Effective Content Promotion: In the realm of content promotion, email marketing stands out as a cost-effective choice. It allows you to reach a broad audience of content consumers without the hefty price tag associated with paid advertising. With a well-crafted email strategy designed for content promotion, you can enjoy impressive returns on investment and increased visibility for your content.

By recognising the paramount importance of building and nurturing your email list within your content marketing strategy, you're strategically positioning your content and brand for long-term success.

Your list becomes a devoted audience eagerly anticipating your valuable content, greatly contributing to your content's reach and influence.

Your Email Sidekick: Email Management and Autoresponders:

Now that you've grasped the significance of building and nurturing your email list, let's chat about your trusty sidekick in this email marketing adventure – email management and autoresponder programs.

So, what exactly are these superhero tools?

Email management and autoresponder programs are like your personal assistants for handling all things email related. They're the ones who help you organise, schedule and send out your emails, making sure they reach the right people at the right time. Think of them as the behind-the-scenes wizards who ensure your email marketing game is on point.

Why should you consider using them?

Well, here's the deal: As your list grows, manually sending out emails to hundreds or thousands of subscribers becomes an impractical and time-consuming task. That's where email management and autoresponder programs swoop in to save the day. They streamline your email marketing efforts, making it a breeze to stay connected with your audience, nurture relationships and deliver your valuable content.

Now, let me tell you about my absolute favourite in this league – Kartra *(for more info on Kartra you can visit my blog at: www.donna-mariecoggins.com/review-of-kartra)*. It's my chosen email management and autoresponder program. With a user-friendly interface and a comprehensive set of features, it's designed to make your life easier. From creating and scheduling emails to automating follow-up sequences, Kartra does it all with finesse.

Kartra is a whole suite of digital marketing tools, with the email and autoresponder part of it being just one feature. So, it's definitely worth checking out.

But you might be thinking, "Is it worth the investment?"

Abso-freaking-lutely! Think of it as an investment in your business's future. The time and effort you'll save by using a top-notch email management and autoresponder program such as Kartra will free you up to focus on what you do best – creating amazing content and serving your audience. Plus, the ROI from well-executed email marketing campaigns can be pretty jaw-dropping. It's like having a 24/7 salesperson working tirelessly to grow your business.

So, don't hesitate to embrace these email superheroes. They'll become your best allies in managing your expanding email list efficiently and taking your content marketing strategy to the next level.

Opt-In Forms: Your Gateways to Success:

Alright, let's dive into the world of opt-in forms, those magical gateways that connect you with your audience and help you grow your email list.

So, what's an opt-in form, you ask?

Well, think of it as your virtual handshake with your potential subscribers. It's a small form placed strategically on your website, blog or landing page that invites visitors to share their contact details with you in exchange for your irresistible lead magnet.

Now, what goes on this form?

Keep it simple and sweet. You'll typically want to ask for their first name and email address. These are the basic building blocks of your email list. Of course, you can get creative and ask for more details down the road, but don't overwhelm them at this stage.

Your opt-in page should be clear, concise and visually appealing. It's all about making a great first impression. Use attention-grabbing headlines and compelling copy that highlight the **benefits** of your lead magnet. Include a captivating image or graphic to make it visually appealing. And don't forget the call-to-action button, guiding them to take that crucial step of subscribing.

Once your new subscriber hits that button, they'll be directed to your Thank You page, the digital equivalent of a warm hug to welcome them to your community.

On this page, you can deliver the promised lead magnet, express your gratitude for joining and set expectations for what they can look forward to from your emails. It's your chance to make them feel valued and excited about their decision to join your tribe.

So, remember, opt-in forms and thank you pages are like the front door to your content kingdom. Make them inviting, friendly and engaging, and you'll pave the way for strong and lasting connections with your audience.

Mastering the Art of Follow-Up:

Effective follow-up is the heartbeat of your email marketing strategy. But we're going to cover this in more detail in a later step. For now, focus on your initial email to your brand new subscribers being one that delivers them the lead magnet that they've just opted-in for.

The Technical Setup:

So, how do you set up this magical opt-in form and automate nurturing follow-up emails?

This is usually a pretty simple process that's done within your email management software – e.g. Kartra, although there are many other programs available too. You can create your opt-in form and your automated email campaign, then either create the opt-in and Thank You pages within your Kartra account or create them on your WordPress site.

Personally, I create these pages on my WordPress site. I copy a little snippet of code from Kartra that is then pasted into where I want my opt-in form to appear on my WordPress site and voila! The opt-in form appears. And when subscribers enter their email address, they're automatically added to my Kartra email system and begin receiving the automated emails.

So, dear friend, consider this chapter your personal guide to mastering the art of lead magnets. You're not just learning about lead magnets; you're becoming a lead magnet maestro, equipped with the knowledge and strategies to turn strangers into subscribers and, eventually, devoted advocates of your brand.

This is your chance to elevate your content marketing strategy from the ordinary to the extraordinary, with the potential to catapult your business to new heights. Well done YOU!

Once you've created your amazing lead magnet and set up your opt-in and Thank You pages, it's time to move on to social media. But this doesn't need to be a time-wasting, soul-sucking experience. In the next chapter, let's look at how to manage our social media, without letting it manage *(or completely take over control of)* us! See you there!

PART 5:
GET SOCIAL

Welcome to **PART 5: GET SOCIAL**, where we're about to embark on an exciting journey into the world of social media. Social media can be a game-changer for your business, but it can also feel overwhelming with the sheer number of platforms and strategies out there. The key is to start with the basics and build from there.

First things first, it's essential to identify where your ideal audience hangs out on social media. You don't need to be everywhere; that's a recipe for burnout.

Instead, focus on 1-2 platforms where your target market is most active. By concentrating your efforts, you can dive deep into mastering the intricacies of these platforms, ensuring your social marketing is both effective and efficient.

Once you've established a strong presence on your chosen platforms, you can consider expanding to a third one if it aligns with your goals and is worth the time investment.

This strategic approach is all about the layering effect, gradually building your social media presence to reach and engage with a broader audience.

In the upcoming chapters, we'll delve deeper into the social media part of your content marketing, providing you with actionable strategies, tips and techniques to make the most of your social content and marketing.

So, Gorgeous, get ready to harness the power of social media to connect with your audience, grow your brand and take your business to the next level.

Chapter 9: Social Media Strategies That Work

Leveraging Social Platforms To Amplify Your Content and Build a Thriving Community

Hello, fellow entrepreneurial adventurer! Welcome to the dynamic world of social media, where the potential to amplify your content and forge meaningful connections with your audience is limitless.

In this chapter, we're delving deep into the intricacies of leveraging social platforms effectively. So, grab your cup of inspiration, get comfortable and let's explore social media strategies that work like a charm for women in business.

The Social Media Landscape: Navigating Opportunities

1. Understanding the Social Media Landscape
Diverse Platforms, Diverse Audiences

Social media isn't a monolithic entity – it's a vibrant tapestry of platforms, each with its own unique characteristics and user demographics. To leverage social media effectively, it's crucial to understand the nuances of major platforms like

Instagram, Facebook, Twitter, LinkedIn, TikTok and Pinterest. Tailoring your approach to fit each platform is the key to reaching a diverse audience.

For example: Instagram, with its emphasis on visually appealing content, might be ideal for a women's fashion brand, while LinkedIn offers a professional space for networking and business-related discussions.

Decoding the Algorithm Enigma

Social media algorithms are like digital maestros, orchestrating the visibility of your content. Staying informed about algorithm changes is vital for maintaining a strong presence. For instance, Instagram's algorithm favours recent posts and high engagement within the first hour, influencing the timing and nature of your content. Posting consistently during peak times and engaging with your audience shortly after posting can positively impact your content's visibility.

2. The Power of Visual Storytelling

Crafting Irresistible Imagery

Humans are visual beings and social media is an image-driven playground. Investing time and effort into creating visually striking images and graphics can significantly enhance your brand's appeal. Share aesthetically pleasing product photos, behind-the-scenes glimpses or create visually appealing quote graphics that align with your brand message.

Embracing the Video Revolution

Video content is increasing across platforms. From short, engaging clips to longer, more in-depth content, videos offer a dynamic way to captivate your audience. They also help to show your personality in a way that images, text and audio can't.

Examples of how you can incorporate videos into your social media content include hosting live Q&A sessions, creating tutorial videos showcasing your expertise or sharing compelling behind-the-scenes videos to humanise your brand.

3. Building a Consistent Brand Presence

Defining Your Brand Voice

Consistency is the cornerstone of brand building. Define your brand voice – how you communicate, the tone you use and the personality you project. Consistent messaging fosters brand recognition and trust. If your brand is known for its playful and quirky personality, for example, infuse humour into your captions and content.

Theme-driven Content

Identify key themes that resonate with your brand and weave them into your content. A cohesive brand story helps reinforce your messaging and values.

Example: If your brand focuses on empowerment, consistently share content that aligns with this theme, such as success stories, motivational quotes and empowering visuals.

4. Strategic Content Distribution
Timing is Everything

Knowing when your audience is most active on each platform ensures your content receives maximum visibility. Understanding peak posting times is crucial for optimising engagement. Thankfully, you can use scheduling tools to post during peak times, ensuring your content appears when your audience is most likely to be online... even if you're not.

The Power of Cross-Promotion

Cross-promoting your content across platforms creates a content loop, maximising your reach and engagement. Sharing your Instagram post on Facebook or your LinkedIn article on Twitter amplifies your content's impact.

For example, share a teaser of your latest blog post on Instagram Stories with a swipe-up link to the full post.

The Heart of Social Media: Engagement and Community Building

1. Authentic Engagement

Responding to Comments

Authentic engagement is the heartbeat of social media success. Responding to comments, answering questions and acknowledging feedback create a genuine connection with your audience.

Respond to comments with personalised messages, thanking your audience for their insights or asking for their thoughts.

Interactive Content Strategies

Using interactive content like polls, quizzes and questions encourages audience participation, turning your social media presence into a two-way conversation.

A good way to do this is to host a poll asking your audience's preference on a new product feature, encouraging them to actively engage with your brand. *(Plus, this helps improve your product creation!)*

2. Community Building Strategies

Private Groups for Exclusivity

Create private community groups on platforms like Facebook. These groups provide an exclusive space for dedicated followers, fostering a sense of belonging and exclusivity.

For example, establish a "VIP Club" for loyal customers, offering exclusive content, early access to promotions and a direct line of communication with your brand.

Harnessing User-Generated Content

Encourage your audience to become content creators themselves. User-generated content not only builds a sense of community but also serves as authentic testimonials for your brand.

One way to do this is to run a contest where participants share photos using your product and feature the best submissions on your social media. Just make sure you follow any rules and regulations that may apply for running contests.

3. Leveraging Influencer Collaborations
Identifying the Right Influencers

Collaborating with influencers whose audience aligns with your ideal client can significantly broaden your reach. Influencers bring authenticity and trust to your brand. For example, if you're in the fitness industry, collaborate with a fitness influencer for product reviews or joint campaigns.

Embracing Micro-Influencers

Consider working with micro-influencers. These are individuals with a smaller but highly engaged following. Micro-influencers often have a niche audience, resulting in more meaningful interactions. A micro-influencer with 5,000 followers might have a more engaged audience than a macro-influencer with 500,000 followers.

4. Using Paid Advertising Effectively
Precision in Targeted Ads

Investing in targeted advertising allows you to reach specific demographics based on interests, behaviour and demographics. This is also a great way to gather data and learn more about what your audience wants, how they react and whether you're on the right track with your offerings.

Analysing Ad Analytics

Monitor ad analytics to understand what resonates with your audience. Use insights to refine your ad strategy and allocate budget effectively. If a particular ad creative performs exceptionally well, consider creating variations with a similar theme for future campaigns.

Measuring Success: Analytics and Key Metrics

1. Social Media Analytics Tools
Platform Insights for In-Depth Understanding

Leverage built-in analytics tools on platforms for valuable insights into your content's performance. These tools provide data on impressions, engagement and follower demographics.

External Analytics for a Comprehensive View

External analytics tools like Google Analytics and Hootsuite offer a broader perspective on your social media performance, integrating data from various platforms.

Track website traffic generated from social media links using Google Analytics, providing insights into user behaviour beyond the platforms.

2. Key Metrics to Monitor

Engagement Rates as a Pulse Check

Track likes, comments, shares and overall engagement. High engagement rates indicate that your content is resonating with your audience. Calculate the engagement rate by dividing total engagement by the number of followers and multiplying by 100.

Follower Growth as an Indicator

Monitor your follower count over time. Consistent growth signifies a healthy and expanding audience. Compare monthly follower growth to identify patterns or spikes, providing insights into the appeal of your content.

Conversion Metrics for Goal Alignment

If your goal is conversion, track metrics like click-through rates *(CTR)* and conversions attributed to social media campaigns. For example, measure the percentage of website visitors from social media who take a desired action, such as making a purchase.

Crafting Your Social Media Magic Wand

1. Personalising Your Approach

Recognise that each platform has its own unique vibe. Tailoring your content to match the tone and expectations of each platform is crucial for optimal engagement. For example, Instagram may be more visual and lifestyle-focused, while LinkedIn requires a more professional tone.

Experimenting with different content types allows you to understand what resonates best with your audience. Flexibility and adaptability are key. Try a mix of carousel posts, video content and infographics to gauge audience preferences.

2. Staying Authentic and Consistent

Authenticity builds trust. Be genuine in your interactions and transparent in your messaging to foster a strong connection with your audience.

One way of doing this is to share behind-the-scenes glimpses of your daily work life or the creative process behind your products. Or share a challenge you're facing and how you're managing it.

Consistency is paramount. Develop a posting schedule and stick to it. Regular content keeps your brand in the minds of your audience. If you decide to post every Monday, Wednesday and Friday, for example, create a content calendar to plan and schedule your posts.

A Word Of Warning:

Another important part of social media marketing is to understand where your ideal client is hanging out. This is where you should be hanging out too. For example, there's no point having perfect content and consistently posting on Pinterest if your ideal clients aren't also using Pinterest.

In most cases, it's not practical to be on all social media platforms, even if your business is a major corporation with a dedicated social media team! So, it's important to choose the one or two where your clients are most likely to be and focus on using them well.

Another important note here is to be careful about how much time you spend on social media. Yes, it's a great way of sharing content and connecting with your clients and potential clients. But... it can also be a huge time-suck!

Perhaps more concerning is the drain it can put on some people's mental health. If you're finding you're spending too long on social media and/or it's having a negative effect on your well-being, act NOW. Do what you can to minimise your time here or even outsource your social media management to someone else. There are professional social media managers who will happily manage your social marketing for you, for a fee.

While social media can be hugely beneficial for your business, it's not worth the cost of your health, my friend. So please make sure you make taking care of your beautiful self a priority too.

A Social Media Symphony for Women in Business

And with that, congratulations, maestro! You've now embarked on a journey to master the art of social media for women in business. Well done you!

Whether you're a solopreneur, a small business owner or a trailblazer in the corporate world, these strategies are your magic wand to amplify your content and build a thriving community.

In the upcoming chapter, we'll delve into the art of building – and nurturing – your tribe. Until then, may your social media journey be as enchanting as a perfectly orchestrated symphony!

Chapter 10: Building Your Tribe: Community Engagement

Fostering a Sense of Community Around Your Brand and Keeping Your Audience Actively Involved

Hello, Beautiful! Welcome to the vibrant world of community building, where your brand transforms into a thriving tribe – a place of shared values, mutual support and everlasting connections.

In this chapter, we're not just scratching the surface; we're diving deep into the essence of community engagement and why it's not just important but utterly transformative for your business.

So, buckle up buttercup! We're about to embark on an exploration of building your tribe and keeping the flame of engagement alive.

The Essence of Community Building

1. Understanding the Power of Community
Community vs. Audience
Let's get real about the difference between an audience and a community. Think of an audience

as your listeners - they're there, but they're not really diving in.

On the other hand, a community? They're your go-getters, the ones who roll up their sleeves and dive into the conversation. It's like the difference between people who just nod along to a podcast and those who actually implement what they learn.

For instance, your audience might give your posts a thumbs up, but your community? They're the ones in the comments, sharing their thoughts, spreading the word and really making your brand feel like everyone's home.

Now, imagine your community as more than just customers – they're your support crew. It's like having a group of friends who are always there to cheer you on.

This is where the magic happens – where people feel like they belong and they're ready to support each other. Picture a fitness brand's community where everyone's sharing tips, celebrating each other's wins and offering a shoulder when the going gets tough.

2. The Role of Community in Brand Loyalty
Building Emotional Connections

Here's where it gets beautiful. A community is not just about buying and selling. It's about shared experiences, emotions and values. It's about creating heart-to-heart connections. Think about a skincare community where everyone's sharing their skin stories and tips. It's not just about buying products; it's about connecting on a deeper level.

Emotional Loyalty vs. Transactional Loyalty
Emotional loyalty is the real deal. It's not just about the transactions; it's about forming an emotional connection that keeps people coming back for more.

It's like when your fashion community shows their love not just by buying your products but by being active in discussions and really connecting with your brand.

Fostering a Vibrant Online Community

1. Choosing the Right Platforms
Tailoring Platforms to Your Community
It's all about finding your community's hangout spot. Different groups shine on different platforms. It's like knowing whether your tribe loves Instagram stories or deep dives into Reddit threads. For example, your tech-savvy folks might be all over Reddit, while your beauty enthusiasts are double-tapping on Instagram.

Multichannel Presence
We're talking about being where your people are. It's like setting up shop in different neighbourhoods. You might have your foodies watching your cooking demos on YouTube, your

photo fans double-tapping on Instagram and your blog readers devouring your latest post.

2. Initiating Community Conversations
Sparks That Ignite Conversations

This is where you get the conversation rolling. Ask those juicy questions that get people talking and sharing. It's like starting a chat at a dinner party that gets everyone leaning in. Maybe your business community is swapping stories about being women in business, sharing both the tough parts and the triumphs.

Polls and Surveys

Get your community in on the decision-making. It's like asking your friends where they want to go for dinner. Maybe your travel buffs are voting on the next group trip destination, making it a real team effort.

3. Encouraging User-Generated Content
Turning Your Audience Into Contributors

This is about shining the spotlight on your community members. Show off their stories, their wins and their journeys. It's like celebrating each person's unique path. Maybe your fitness buffs are posting their workout victories, inspiring everyone in the group.

Contests and Challenges

It's time to get creative! Host a challenge or a contest that gets everyone involved. It's like throwing a party where everyone gets to show off their best dance moves. Your photography enthusiasts, for example, could be snapping away at a monthly theme challenge, each bringing their own flair.

Nurturing Your Tribe's Growth

1. Providing Value Through Educational Content

The Power of Continuous Learning

Let's talk growth. Hosting webinars or workshops is like inviting your community to a classroom where everyone's eager to learn. Imagine your marketing peeps tuning into a webinar about the latest trends, soaking up all that knowledge.

Sharing Educational Resources

It's about giving your community the tools to grow. Share those articles, guides and resources that help everyone level up. It's like handing out the best books to your book club. Your writers could be sharing writing tips and resources, helping each other polish their craft.

2. Facilitating Peer-to-Peer Connections
Connecting Like Minds

Introducing your community members to each other is so exciting. It's like being the host who knows just who should talk to whom at a party. Maybe your parenting community is linking up parents facing similar challenges, creating a network of support.

Themed Networking Events

Throw a themed networking event – this is similar to a themed party where everyone has something in common. Maybe your business folks are mingling at a virtual event for entrepreneurs, making connections that matter. I attended one of these recently and it was so much fun as we all got into character for the event! And of course, it was worthwhile for business and connections too. But, oh so much fun!

3. Recognising and Celebrating Milestones
Making Every Win Count

Celebrating your community's milestones is well worth the effort – it's a big deal. Maybe your book club is having a virtual party for its first anniversary, making everyone feel special and appreciated. Or perhaps one of your writing students just published their first book. Yay! Celebrate with them and get the whole community involved.

This is especially powerful when your community members may not have others around them who encourage and support them, sharing their victories... especially small ones. The support they get from their community may make all the difference between them achieving their goals or giving up.

Member Spotlights

Let's give a shoutout to your community stars. It's like giving a standing ovation to someone who's really made a difference. An art community might spotlight their "Artist of the Month," inspiring everyone with their creativity.

Keeping the Flame Alive: Sustaining Community Engagement

1. Consistent and Transparent Communication
The Glue That Binds

Stay in touch with your community. Regular updates and open conversations build trust and keep everyone in the loop. It's like keeping your friends updated with what's going on in your life. For example, a software community might be all about sharing the latest feature updates and getting everyone excited.

Addressing Concerns Promptly

It's important to listen and respond quickly when your community has concerns. This shows you care and that you're there for them. It's like when a friend needs advice and you're right there to help. A customer support community might be on top of product questions, showing they're all about solutions.

2. Creating Community Guidelines
Setting the Tone for Healthy Interaction

Setting clear guidelines is like laying down house rules for a party. It ensures everyone plays nice and has a good time. A wellness community might set rules for respectful, supportive discussions, making sure it's a safe space for everyone.

Some community platforms, such as Facebook Groups, give you examples of group rules you can apply when setting up your group. When a new member requests to join, they'll need to tick the box to say they've read and agree to those rules first.

Moderation and Conflict Resolution

Having moderators is like having bouncers at your party – they keep things smooth and handle any hiccups. A gaming community, for example, might have moderators to make sure everyone's playing fair and having fun.

3. Embracing Feedback and Iteration
Evolving With Your Community

When managing your community, it's good to encourage and be open to feedback, whether you like it or not. Just like asking your friends for advice – it shows you value their opinions and want to keep improving. Maybe your software users are giving input that helps make your app even better.

Adapting to Changing Needs

Stay flexible and ready to evolve with your community's needs. Think of it as changing up the music at a party when you see the vibe shifting. A fashion community, for instance, might switch up their discussion topics to keep up with what's trending.

Measuring Community Engagement Success

1. Analysing Community Metrics
Beyond Vanity Metrics

Keeping an eye on likes, comments and shares helps you understand how much your community is engaging. It's kind of like noticing who's chatting and who's just nodding along at your party. Your photographers might be tracking engagement on their latest snaps, seeing who's really connecting.

Participation Levels

Measuring how often and how deeply your members engage helps you get the pulse of your community. It's like checking who's really getting into the discussions at your book club and who's just there for the snacks.

Some people are 'lurkers' – they like to look and listen but rarely participate. When you notice who's doing this, gently encourage them to participate. Don't necessarily call them out but share a post specifically for the lurkers to let them know it's a safe place for them to get involved too.

2. Qualitative Feedback and Sentiment Analysis

Gauging Member Satisfaction

Using surveys and feedback forms is a good way to gauge member satisfaction. Think of this as asking your friends for their honest thoughts after a get-together. Maybe your travellers are giving feedback on their latest virtual trip, helping you plan even better ones in the future.

Sentiment Analysis Tools

Sentiment analysis tools help you capture the mood of your community. They help you to read your community, similar to reading the room to see if everyone's enjoying the party. A gaming community, for example, might use these tools to see how everyone feels about the latest game update.

Crafting Your Tribe's Legacy

1. Documenting Community Stories
Chronicles of Connection
Have you ever created a scrapbook of photos to help remember all the great times you've had with a particular person, group of people or maybe a special holiday? I love these types of things and so do many others.

So, compiling your community's stories is a brilliant way to capture the essence of community experiences. Maybe your foodies are putting together a cookbook with everyone's favourite recipes, sharing a piece of their world. *(Do you have any idea how popular the Queensland Country Women's Association's cookbooks are? HUGE! Many of my favourite recipes come from this book.)*

Celebrating Community Anniversaries
Celebrating your community's anniversaries is like marking important milestones in a friendship and a great way to encourage community involvement. For example, a photography group might create a special montage to commemorate their journey together, capturing all the memorable moments.

2. Honouring Community Champions
Recognising Contributions

Think of giving out awards as being akin to giving a high-five to those who've really made an impact. Maybe your writers are celebrating with awards for the best stories or most supportive members, acknowledging their star players. The awards don't need to cost much. It could be a digital certificate, a token gift or even a discount on their next purchase from you.

Member Hall of Fame

Just like framing your favourite photos, creating a hall of fame is a great way to remember and honour the best moments and contributors. A fitness community, for example, might have a special section on their website for those who've hit major milestones, celebrating their hard work and dedication.

Your Tribe, Your Legacy

Congratulations, visionary leader! You've embarked on a transformative journey to not just build a brand but to nurture a vibrant community – a tribe that thrives on connection, support and shared experiences.

As we wrap up this chapter, let's remember that your tribe isn't just a collection of individuals. It's so much more! It's a living, breathing entity with its own stories, victories and legacy. And your tribe – your community – will have your back whenever you need them, so long as you're looking out for their best interests too.

In the next chapter, we'll explore the art of SEO – Search Engine Optimisation. Until then, may your tribe continue to flourish and leave an indelible mark on the world!

PART 6: PROMOTION

Welcome to **PART 6: PROMOTION**, a crucial piece of the content marketing puzzle. You see, creating fantastic content is just the first step. To truly make an impact, you must also promote it effectively. This is the bridge that separates those whose content remains hidden from the world and those whose content is adored by thousands, hundreds of thousands or even millions of people.

Start by sharing your content on your social media platforms, as we discussed in **PART 5: GET SOCIAL.** It's a fantastic way to get the word out and connect with your audience. But don't stop there; add one more promotion strategy into the mix. Just one, for now. Later, you can incorporate additional strategies.

Now, let's address a common misconception: some folks believe that content marketing doesn't work. I can tell you from experience, along with a heap of stats and other people's success, that's complete phooey.

There are two primary reasons for this misconception:
1. They're not promoting their content enough or not at all.

2. They give up too soon. It's akin to trying to get in shape by eating well for a day or hitting the gym once and then quitting because they don't see immediate results.

Here's the truth: content marketing works, but it operates on a compounding principle. It takes time and consistency to see the snowball effect. Stay committed, even when you don't see instant results, and you'll begin to witness the magic of your efforts multiplying over time.

So, my lovely, get ready to supercharge your content marketing by mastering the art of promotion and reaping the rewards of your dedication.

Chapter 11: SEO Simplified: Boosting Visibility and Reach

Demystifying Search Engine Optimisation to Ensure Your Content Gets Discovered

Hello, savvy business owner! Ready to unlock the secrets of SEO and propel your content into the spotlight?

Great!

In this chapter, we're embarking on a comprehensive journey through the intricacies of Search Engine Optimisation. I'll guide you through the ABCs of SEO, delve into the nitty-gritty of crafting SEO-friendly content and equip you with tools and techniques to measure your success.

So, buckle up for an in-depth exploration where we demystify SEO, making it not just understandable but actionable for your content marketing strategy.

The ABCs of SEO: An Overview

1. Decoding SEO: A User-Friendly Approach
Navigating the SEO Landscape

What is SEO, really? Search Engine Optimisation is not a mystical chant – it's about making your content discoverable. Imagine it as a roadmap that guides search engines, such as Google.com, to your content when users are looking for specific information. For example, picture someone in New York searching for "best cupcakes." Effective SEO ensures that if you're a local New York bakery with delightful cupcakes, you appear in their search results.

When talking about SEO we also refer to **User Intent**. This is your North Star of SEO.

At the heart of SEO is understanding what users are searching for – their intent. Google's algorithms aim to provide results that satisfy user queries.

For example, if someone searches for "healthy cookie recipes," your aim is for your blog post about nutritious cookie alternatives should be a top result. Whereas if someone searched for "apple", the search engines will try to determine the user's intent such as, do they want to buy an apple to eat? Or are they looking for an Apple product, such as an iPhone or Mac? And your goal is for your content to make it crystal clear what your content is about.

2. The Power of Keywords: Your Content's BFFs *(BFF=Best Friend Forever... just in case you were wondering.)*

Crafting a Keyword Strategy

The first step in crafting your keyword strategy is to choose the right keywords – or key phrases. Select keywords that align with your content and match the user intent. Strategic keyword strategy is your key to getting your content found.

Try to narrow your keywords to be found by your ideal clients. For example, if you're in the fitness industry, using the keyword of 'fitness' is too broad. Yes, you may be found by more people, providing you can be found amongst all the competition for this broad term. But you're going to be attracting a lot of people who aren't your ideal client. It's much more effective for you to be more specific, using keywords such as 'home workouts for new mums' or something else relevant, that's more specific for your ideal client.

These longer, more specific keyphrases are known as **long-tail keywords** and these are your secret weapon! Leveraging long-tail keywords, the specific phrases that capture niche searchers, can lead to higher conversion rates as they align closely with user intent.

SEO-Friendly Content Creation

1. Crafting Compelling Content That Google Loves

The Marriage of Quality and Relevance

Once you've chosen specific keyphrases to use with your content, the foundation of good optimisation is having **quality content**.

Here's the thing: Google rewards high-quality, informative and engaging content. The emphasis is on providing value to the user.

Let's say you offer in-depth guides on photography techniques, Google *(and other search engines)* recognises your expertise and may rank your content higher in the search results when a potential customer searches on terms related to your content.

The next thing to focus on to flaunt what you've got in the search engines is **relevance**. This is like the content GPS for Google and co.

Align your content with user intent and weave your target keywords naturally. It's not just about having quality content but making sure it's what users are looking for.

Let's use the example of a life coach. A good SEO strategy may be to create content addressing common challenges with keywords like "overcoming self-doubt." Providing this is something you help your clients with and want to be found for, of course.

2. Optimising On-Page Elements: The Art of Fine-Tuning

Title Tags, Meta Descriptions and More

Title tags are your headline heroes. So, craft compelling titles that incorporate target keywords and entice clicks. Your title is the first thing users see in search results and this is followed by a very brief description of the content – your **meta description**.

Your meta description is a mini preview. It should summarise your content, again including the keyphrase you're optimising this piece of content for. This is your chance to give users a glimpse of what your content offers.

Together, the aim of your title and meta description is to make searchers want to learn more. Which means, they click the link and visit the page with your content on it.

Next is your **header tags** – your content's skeleton. These are referred to as H1, H2, H3 and so on and are used to structure your content. This not only makes it more readable for users but also helps search engines understand the hierarchy of information. For example, you could use H1 tags for your blog post title and H2 tags for sub-headings.

Technical SEO Demystified

1. Behind the Scenes: The Technical Wizardry
Site Structure

Consider Site Structure the blueprint of user experience. It's important to organise your site logically for easy navigation. A well-structured site enhances user experience and makes it easier for search engines to crawl.

To do this for your blog, clearly categorise blog topics like "Healthy Recipes," "Fitness Tips," and "Wellness Insights." And make sure your site is easy to navigate. In fact, it's worth asking your customers for their feedback on any issues they've had or suggestions on how your site's navigation could be improved.

Mobile Friendliness and Speed

We are in a mobile-first era, my friend. Google prioritises mobile-friendly sites. So, it's essential that your content shines on smartphones and tablets to cater to the growing mobile audience. Make sure you optimise images for mobile, use responsive design and regularly test your site's mobile friendliness.

Page speed is also important and something that search engines consider when ranking where your content should appear within the search engines.

Why?

Because people want web pages to load quickly. If the page takes too long to show the content, they'll go back to the search results and click to go to another site. So, Google likes to reward fast page load speeds because you're giving searchers what they want. Capiche?

In short, users "bounce" *(that is, they leave straight away)* if your site takes too long to load. Optimise images, leverage browser caching and consider content delivery networks for swift loading.

At the time of writing this, the goal is for your page to load in under three seconds to retain user interest.

If you're not sure how to do any of these techie tasks, don't stress and don't waste hours learning it. Delegate this to a decent website developer and they'll easily look after it for you. You've got more important ways to spend your time that learning this if it's not your area of expertise.

2. Backlinks: The Popularity Contest
Building Authority Through Quality Links

In simple terms, a backlink is when a site recommends your site – or page – by adding a link back to your content on its site. This is good for SEO because it shows the search engines that another site thinks your content is worth recommending, so it's probably quality content worth recommending to searchers.

Focus on getting high-quality backlinks from reputable sources keeping in mind you always want quality over quantity. Make this your backlink mantra. A single high-quality link can outweigh numerous low-quality ones. In particularly, links from government and educational sites tend to be highly rated.

An example of this is when a well-established fitness magazine includes a link to your workout routine article. This goes a long way to enhance your content's credibility and the search engines take notice of this.

The thing is, if you want to focus on getting links back to your content, it's important to focus on natural link building. This is a slow process, but worth the effort. If you try to shortcut and 'cheat' the search engines, they'll notice. And you may end up ranking far lower in the search results as a result.

So, cultivate natural links by creating shareable, valuable content that others want to reference. Quality content naturally attracts links. If you provide groundbreaking insights in your industry, for example, other blogs may naturally link to your research.

Measuring SEO Success
1. Analysing Metrics Beyond Rankings
Metrics That Matter

When it comes to measuring your SEO success, it's important to know and focus on metrics that matter.

So, just what are the metrics that matter? Here's are the two most important SEO metrics to focus on:

- **Organic Traffic: The Heartbeat of SEO**
  o Monitor the growth of organic traffic over time. A steady increase indicates that your content is becoming more visible and reaching a larger audience.
- **Conversion Rates: Turning Clicks Into Action**
  o Track how many visitors take desired actions, such as signing up for newsletters or making purchases. This indicates the effectiveness of your content engagement.
  o *Example: If your goal is newsletter sign-ups, a rising conversion rate shows that your content is resonating with your audience. Similarly, if your goal is to increase sales then you want to see a direct increase in sales, linked to your organic traffic.*

2. Tools for SEO Mastery

Navigating the SEO Toolbox

There are two main tools you'll want to use to help you navigate SEO. These are:

- **Google Analytics: Your Data Ally**

  Leverage Google Analytics for in-depth insights into user behaviour, traffic sources and so much more. Understand what's working and do more of it!

  Google Analytics is a free tool that you can use after getting your web developer to integrate it with your Home Base – i.e. your WordPress blog. Once installed and collecting data, you'll be able to easily see all sorts of valuable stats such as how many people visit which pages on your site, how long they stay, how they found your content *(e.g. Facebook, organic, referral, etc),* what browser they're using, whether they're using a PC or mobile device and so much more. This is so useful in helping you to know what's working, and what isn't, as well as information that can help you to better tailor your content and its delivery.

- **Keyword Research Tools: Your Compass in the SEO Jungle**

  Use tools like Ahrefs, SEMrush or Google Keyword Planner to refine your keyword strategy. These are worthwhile to help you stay ahead of trends and optimise your content accordingly.

The Ever-Evolving SEO Landscape

1. Staying Ahead in a Dynamic Environment
Adaptation and Future Trends

In the world of SEO, staying informed about search engine algorithm updates is key. Just like fashion trends, search engines keep changing what they love. One day it's all about one thing, and the next, it's something else. Take Google's Page Experience Update, for instance. It's all about user experience now, and that's what's going to help your site shine in the rankings.

So, it's important to stay up to date on what's happening in SEO-land. *(Hint: follow-my blog at https://Donna-MarieCoggins.com/blog for major updates and changes.)*

Voice Search

Now, let's chat about voice search. It's the new kid on the block. Optimising for voice search means thinking about how people really talk. Imagine someone asking their phone, "Hey Google, find the best yoga studios near me."

Your content needs to be that friend who answers back in a natural, helpful way, so write in a way that your ideal customer speaks. Use their style of words and write in short sentences. This will help the search engines to recommend your content when it best matches relevant voice searches.

2. Common SEO Pitfalls: A Survival Guide
Keyword Stuffing

When it comes to keywords, think of them like sprinkles on a cupcake – a little goes a long way. Google wants your content to flow like a nice chat over coffee, not like a robot. So, remember, you're writing for real people who want to read something genuine. You don't want to keyword stuff, which is, as it sounds – stuffing in as many keywords as you can. Keep it natural, use synonyms and mix it up. Your readers – and Google – will thank you for it.

Ignoring Mobile Optimisation: A Critical Oversight

In today's world, if your site isn't friendly to smartphone users, it's like having a party and forgetting to invite at least half your friends. More and more people are browsing on their phones, so making your site mobile-friendly is a must. Don't miss out on reaching those on-the-go readers. And viewers. And listeners.

Crafting Your SEO Success Story

1. Building a Strong Foundation for Sustainable Growth
Your SEO Roadmap

- **Consistency: The Bedrock of SEO**
  Consistency in SEO is like watering your plants – do it regularly and you'll see them

bloom. Keep your content fresh and updated. Google loves it and so will your community. This is one reason why a blog is a must-have on your website. Having a blog makes it easy for you to add new content regularly. This is all about showing Google and your readers that you're here to stay and always have something new to share.

- **Adaptation: Embracing the SEO Journey**

SEO is a journey, not a destination. It's like being a surfer; you need to ride the waves and adjust to the changing tides. What works today might need a tweak tomorrow. So, if a new competitor shows up, don't sweat it. Take a peek at what they're doing and see if you can learn from it. It's all about staying flexible and riding that SEO wave.

Your SEO Adventure Begins

Congratulations, darling friend! You've armed yourself with the knowledge, strategies and a roadmap for SEO success.

Now, there are more things you can do to optimise your content but getting the hang of what we've covered in this chapter – and doing it consistently – covers all the basics to give you a head start and increase your visibility within the search engines.

As we conclude this chapter, remember that SEO isn't a one-time fix; it's an ongoing journey. Keep honing your skills, stay informed about industry changes and watch your content soar to new heights in search engine rankings.

In the next chapter, we'll delve into the art of crafting effective emails that build relationships and take your business to the next level – email marketing magic. Until then, happy optimising!

Chapter 12: Email Marketing Magic: Connecting Directly with Your Audience

Crafting Effective Email Campaigns that Build Relationships and Drive Business Growth

Hey there, my beautiful friend! Today, we're unlocking the secrets of Email Marketing – where every email is a chance to connect, engage and weave a web of magic that captivates your audience.

So, grab your favourite cuppa, settle into your cozy reading spot and let's dive deep into the realm of crafting emails that not only land in your audience's inbox but also create lasting connections. Welcome to the wizardry of Email Marketing!

The Power of Email Marketing

1. Why Email? Unveiling the Superpowers
A Direct Line to Your Audience

Email isn't just a tool; it's a direct line to the beating heart of your audience. It's the secret ingredient that turns one-time customers into lifelong fans. Think of it as a personal invitation into the world of your brand, where every subscriber is greeted by name, creating an immediate and intimate connection.

Unlike the unpredictable landscape of social media algorithms, your email list is a sanctuary you mostly control. It's a digital haven where your messages can land directly in your audience's inbox, bypassing the noise and ensuring your voice is heard.

2. The ROI Wonder: Email vs. Other Channels
Dollars and Sense

Let's talk about the financial magic of Email Marketing. For every dollar you invest, the average return is a staggering $42. Email consistently outperforms other marketing channels, showcasing its prowess in converting subscribers into paying customers. Craft your campaigns with clear calls-to-action, and you're not just sending emails – you're making a wise investment in your business growth.

Building Your Email List

1. The Foundation: A Stellar Opt-In Incentive
Enticing Subscribers to Join

Building a robust email list starts with an irresistible opt-in incentive, also known as your Lead Magnet, which we discussed in **PART 4:**

LEAD MAGNET. This is the golden ticket that persuades visitors to become subscribers. Whether it's an exclusive ebook, a VIP webinar or a special discount, your incentive should be a tantalising offer your ideal clients can't resist.

Crafting clear and compelling calls-to-action *(CTAs)* across your website and social media is key. Make it easy for potential subscribers to take that leap into your email community. By offering a valuable incentive, you're not just growing a list; you're building a community of engaged and interested individuals.

2. Segmentation: The Key to Personalisation
Tailoring Content for Maximum Impact

Now that your list is flourishing, let's talk about segmentation – an art that brings personalisation to the forefront. By understanding your audience's preferences, demographics or purchase history, you can create segments that receive tailored content.

Why does this matter?

Simple... because personalised content resonates.

Imagine sending a special promotion on athletic wear to subscribers who have shown interest in fitness-related content. Then compare that to receiving an email about something you have zero interest in. There's a big difference, right?

So, it's not just an email you're sending. It's a personalised experience that enhances engagement and connection.

Crafting Irresistible Email Campaigns

1. The Art of the Welcome Series
Rolling Out the Red Carpet for New Subscribers

First impressions matter, especially in the world of Email Marketing. A welcome series is like rolling out the red carpet for new subscribers. It's a sequence of emails designed to introduce your brand, share your values and set the tone for what subscribers can expect.

But it's not just about one-way communication. Encourage interaction from the start. Whether it's prompting replies, conducting surveys or inviting them to connect on social media, make it a two-way street. A welcome series isn't just about greetings; it's about building a community from the get-go.

2. Nurturing Campaigns: Turning Subscribers into Fans
Building Lasting Relationships

Nurturing campaigns are the heartbeat of your Email Marketing strategy. They're the gradual unveiling of what makes your brand special. Drip campaigns, where you share valuable content, insights and exclusive offers over a series of emails, are your secret weapon.

What's the key to effective nurturing?
Providing value in every email. Whether it's educational content, entertaining stories or exclusive perks, make sure each email enriches your subscribers' experience. Share success stories, tips or behind-the-scenes glimpses to keep them engaged and looking forward to your emails.

Email Copywriting Mastery

1. Subject Line Sorcery
Making Your Emails Irresistible to Open
Your subject line is the gateway to your emails. Craft lines that not only grab attention but also pique curiosity. Personalise them to make your subscribers feel seen and valued. Subject lines like "Unlock Your Secret Surprise Inside" or "Exclusive Access: Your VIP Pass Awaits!" create an immediate sense of intrigue.

> **The aim of your subject line is to encourage recipients to open and read the email.**

2. Compelling Body Copy: Storytelling and Engagement
Keeping Subscribers Hooked
Your email's body copy is where the magic truly happens. It's the space where you weave compelling narratives that captivate and

emotionally resonate with your subscribers. Share customer success stories, your personal journey or anecdotes related to your products or services.

Strategically place calls to action *(CTAs)* throughout your email. What's the next logical step you want subscribers to do after reading your email?

Whether it's guiding subscribers to explore more content, make a purchase or engage with your brand, a well-placed CTA ensures your emails aren't just stories – they're invitations to take action.

And that's one of the goals of your email body – to encourage readers to take action. The other goal is to build a relationship and build trust with your subscribers.

The Science of Email Timing and Frequency

1. Finding the Sweet Spot: When to Hit Send
Timing Matters

Timing can make or break your email's impact. Understand your audience's habits. Analyse data to identify when they're most active and likely to engage with emails. Testing and iterating are your allies in refining the timing for optimal engagement.

There used to be 'best days' and 'best times' to send emails, but I've found that now varies greatly from one niche to another. So, it's always worth testing for YOUR particular market.

2. Balancing Act: Email Frequency
Staying Present Without Overwhelming
Consistency is the heartbeat of successful email marketing. Find a frequency that suits your audience and stick to it. If sending weekly newsletters, ensure they consistently land in subscribers' inboxes on the same day and time each week.

Monitor engagement metrics. If you notice a decline, consider adjusting frequency or altering the content strategy. Your goal is to stay present without overwhelming your subscribers, creating a steady rhythm that keeps your brand top of mind.

Harnessing the Power of Analytics

1. Data-Driven Decisions: Analytics Unveiled
Leveraging Insights for Optimisation
Email marketing isn't just an art; it's a science. Analytics provide the clues to optimise your strategy. Open rates are your first indicator of email success. Craft subject lines that resonate and analyse open rates to understand subscriber preferences. A good email management program will have reports available to make it easy to see these sorts of stats.

My personal preference for my email management is Kartra *(refer this post on my blog for more details: www.donna-mariecoggins.com/review-of-kartra)* and I absolutely love it. If you're already using something else and you're happy with it – and it can do all you need it to – great! Stay with it. But if not, have a look at Kartra.

Click-through rates *(CTR)* indicate how many subscribers are taking desired actions by clicking the links in your emails. That's where the term gets its name from... people **Click Through** to whatever it is the link takes them to.

Track the performance of different CTAs and content types to optimise for higher engagement. Data-driven decisions ensure your email campaigns evolve and adapt to meet your audience's changing preferences.

2. Subscriber Feedback: A Treasure Trove
Listening to Your Audience

Your subscribers hold the key to unlocking the full potential of your email marketing strategy. Encourage them to provide feedback through surveys or by responding directly to your emails. Ask for input on content preferences, frequency or any specific topics they'd like covered.

It's also essential to analyse unsubscribes and email bounces to understand potential issues and refine your strategy. Every piece of feedback is a gem, guiding you towards creating content that resonates and strengthens your connection with your audience.

Staying Compliant: The ABCs of Email Regulations

1. Navigating Legal Waters: Email Compliance
Building Trust Through Transparency

Email marketing isn't just about creativity; it's about responsibility. Building trust through transparency is crucial. Ensure subscribers have willingly opted in to receive emails. Clearly communicate the benefits of subscribing and set expectations about the type of content they'll receive.

Include a clear and easy-to-find unsubscribe option in every email. Respecting your subscribers' choices is not just good practice, it's a legal requirement. By adhering to email regulations like CAN-SPAM, you're not only building trust but also maintaining the integrity of your email marketing strategy.

If you're sending emails to anyone located within Europe, GDPR regulations may also apply. A good email management system can help you make sure you're adhering to regulations in this regard, too. For example, using Kartra allows me select GDPR option in the main setup. Then, whenever someone subscribes to my list from a location where GDPR regulations apply, they are shown the necessary information to agree to receive emails from me. So basically, Kartra looks after it all for me.

The Symbiosis of Email and Content Marketing

So, why should Email Marketing be an integral part of your content marketing strategy? It's the symbiotic relationship that ensures your carefully crafted content doesn't just exist; it thrives. Here are the main benefits:

1. Amplifying Your Content Reach
Taking Your Content Further
Your blog posts, videos and podcasts are valuable assets, but they need wings to soar. Email marketing gives your content the boost it deserves. By sharing your latest creations directly with your subscribers, you amplify your reach and ensure your content doesn't get lost in the vast online landscape.

2. Building Deeper Connections
Beyond Clicks and Views
Emails are more than just vehicles for content delivery; they're a medium for building genuine connections. Through personalised emails, you're not just addressing your audience; you're having a one-on-one conversation. This personal

touch goes beyond clicks and views – it builds relationships.

3. Driving Action with Strategic Emails
Moving Beyond Awareness

Content marketing creates awareness, but Email Marketing takes it a step further. Through strategic emails, you guide your audience to take specific actions – whether it's exploring more content, making a purchase or engaging with your brand on social media. It's the bridge that turns passive readers into active participants.

4. Data-Driven Optimisation
Evolving with Your Audience

The beauty of integrating Email Marketing into your content strategy is the wealth of data it provides. Analysing email metrics helps you understand what resonates with your audience. From open rates to click-through rates, every data point is a clue guiding you towards refining and optimising your content strategy.

Your Email Magic Journey Continues

Congratulations, magical marketer! You've embarked on a journey into the realms of Email Marketing, armed with spells to captivate and engage your audience. As we wrap up this chapter, remember that Email Marketing is a dynamic dance of strategy, creativity and continuous improvement.

In the upcoming chapter, we'll delve into the realm of ***Collaborations and Partnerships: Amplifying Your Reach***, where we're going to explore the exciting world of collaborative growth. This chapter is all about the power of joining forces with others in your industry.

We'll dive into how strategic partnerships and collaborations can significantly expand your reach, bring fresh perspectives, and open up new avenues for mutual growth. Get ready to discover how connecting with like-minded individuals and businesses can transform your content journey and take your success to new heights!

Until then, keep the magic alive in your emails, and may your campaigns sparkle with success!

Chapter 13: Collaborations and Partnerships: Amplifying Your Reach

Unleashing the Magic of Working Together for Growth

Hello, beautiful friend! Today, we're diving into one of my favourite topics – collaborations and partnerships.

Imagine it's like joining forces with your business besties to create something extraordinary. So, let's chat over a cup of coffee *(or your favourite tea)* about how teaming up with others can take your business to incredible new heights.

Why Collaborations Are Like Business Superfood

Collaborations are not just nice-to-haves. They're incredibly powerful growth engines for your business.

Friendly Stat Alert: Did you know that companies focusing on collaboration are five times more likely to be high performing? That's a big deal!

The Sweet Spot of Collaboration

1. **Reach New Audiences:** Collaborations open doors to new, engaged audiences who are just waiting to fall in love with your brand.

2. **Fresh Ideas on Tap:** When you collaborate, you're essentially brainstorming with a buddy who brings a whole new perspective.

3. **Sharing is Caring *(and Cost-Effective!)*:** Pooling resources can save you money and time – and who doesn't love that?

4. **Boost Your Brand's Trust Factor:** When another brand vouches for you, their audience listens. It's like getting a five-star review in front of a whole new crowd.

Finding Your Collaboration Soulmate

Think of finding the right partner like matchmaking for your business.

Tips for Perfect Pairing:

- **Values Are Vital:** Your ideal partner should share similar values and ethos. It's like having shared life goals in a relationship.

- **Complementary, Not Competing:** Look for businesses that complement yours. Think peanut butter and jelly – different but oh-so-good together.

- **The Win-Win Wonderland:** Both parties should come out smiling. Make sure the collaboration benefits both of you, as well as your customers.

Collaboration Success Story:

One of the most successful business collaborations I've ever seen was in a small regional town in Queensland, Australia, in the early days of my business. A group of businesses who all catered to the wedding industry teamed up to cross-promote each other with great success. There were dozens of businesses involved in this and, as well as recommending each other and having a good relationship when working together with clients, they often advertised together, sharing the cost. They even created printed marketing materials such as a glossy colour brochure featuring each of their businesses.

Another great example of this was a health food blogger who teamed up with an organic grocery store. They co-create a series of recipe videos featuring the store's products. The blogger gets to reach foodies who shop at the store and the store taps into the blogger's health-conscious followers. It's a match made in heaven!

Types of Collaborations to Spark Your Imagination

Let's explore some of the various ways you can collaborate to make your business shine.

1. **Joint Ventures:** Maybe it's a combined product or a shared service. Think of it as creating a limited edition 'best of both worlds' offer.
2. **Affiliate Love:** Promote each other's products and share the love *(and the profits)*.
3. **Content Buddies:** Create blogs, podcasts or social media content together. It's double the fun and double the reach.
4. **Event Magic:** Host a webinar, workshop or even a retreat together. It's like throwing a party where everyone learns something valuable.
5. **Social Media Swap:** Take over each other's Instagram or Facebook for a day. It's a fun way to introduce yourself to a whole new audience.

Crafting a Collaboration Strategy That Sparkles

A successful collaboration needs a thoughtful strategy, much like planning a fabulous event.

1. **Define Your Goals:** Are you looking to increase your email list, boost brand awareness or drive sales? Set clear targets.
2. **Communication is Your BFF:** Keep the lines open and check in regularly. It keeps everyone on the same page and builds a strong relationship.
3. **Get It in Writing:** A little paperwork can save a lot of headaches later. Outline expectations, roles and responsibilities.

Real-Life Strategy Win:

Anna, a yoga instructor, partnered with a wellness app for a series of virtual classes. They set clear goals for user sign-ups and regularly communicated to tweak their strategy. *The result?* A 52% increase in app subscriptions and a boost in Anna's online following.

Navigating the Collaboration Journey

Every collaboration can teach you something valuable, even if there are a few bumps along the way.

Smooth Sailing Tips:

- **Clarity is Queen:** Be clear about what you're bringing to the table and what you expect in return.

- **Adapt and Grow:** Be open to adjusting your plans. Sometimes, the best results come from unexpected detours.
- **Resolving Ripples:** If issues arise, tackle them with a problem-solving hat on. It's all about finding solutions together.

Measuring the Success of Your Team Effort

Just like in any aspect of your business, you want to know how well your collaboration is performing.

- **KPIs *(Key Performance Indicators)* Really Are Key:** Whether it's new followers, webinar attendees or sales numbers, track what matters.
- **Reflection Time:** After the collaboration, take time to reflect. What lessons can you carry into your next partnership?

Celebrating Success:
   A boutique owner and a local artist collaborated on a line of hand-painted clothing. They tracked their sales and social media buzz, finding an increase in store traffic of over 40% and a wave of new Instagram followers. Cheers to that!

Wrapping Up with a Bow

Remember, collaborations are not just about business growth; they're about building relationships and learning from each other. They add that extra sparkle to your business journey.

Your Next Step: Start brainstorming potential collaborators who align with your brand. Draft a proposal and reach out. Your next amazing collaboration is just around the corner!

In our next chapter, we'll explore *Analytics and Insights: Measuring Your Content Success*. Here, we're going to delve into the exciting world of data and analytics. *(Yes, it really CAN be exciting!)*

This chapter is all about interpreting data to understand what's really resonating with your audience. We'll explore how to use insights to refine your content strategy for even better results. So, gear up, my friend, to discover the power of data in amplifying your content's impact and success!

PART 7:
ADVANCED
STRATEGIES

Welcome to **PART 7: ADVANCED STRATEGIES**, where we'll dive deep into the finer intricacies of content marketing.

By now, you've built a strong foundation, mastered the art of lead magnets, discovered the power of email marketing and explored effective promotion strategies. Congratulations, Lovely! Give yourself a big pat on the back because you're well on your way to content marketing success. But there's more to learn and explore on this exciting journey.

In the chapters ahead, we'll unlock the power of Analytics and Insights: Measuring Your Content Success. Understanding the data behind your content is like having a secret decoder ring that helps you make informed decisions and fine-tune your strategies. You'll learn how to track your content's performance, decipher meaningful insights and use data-driven decisions to amplify your impact.

Plus, we'll delve into the art of Content Repurposing, a game-changer for content creators. Discover how to take one piece of content and transform it into multiple formats, extending its reach and maximising your efforts. Repurposing allows you to get more mileage out of your content while catering to various audience preferences.

In this section, you'll also discover the power of content planning and calendars – how organising is going to be the best way for you to stay consistent. This is going to be important for you because consistency is the bedrock of successful content marketing. You'll explore how to create a content calendar, strategise your content production and maintain a steady flow of valuable content. Not only does this keep your audience engaged but it also establishes your brand as a reliable source of information.

Lastly, we'll address an essential topic that every content creator faces: Overcoming Content Burnout. Self-care strategies are vital to ensure you maintain your creative spark and passion for content creation. We'll delve into effective ways to prevent burnout, stay inspired and continue producing exceptional content.

As you set off on this advanced leg of your content marketing journey, remember that each chapter is a stepping stone toward becoming a content marketing maestro.

Embrace these strategies, put them into action and watch your content marketing efforts soar to new heights.

So, let's dive into PART 7 and unlock the secrets of advanced content marketing together!

Chapter 14: Analytics And Insights: Measuring Your Content Success

Interpreting Data to Refine Your Strategy for Better Results

Hello, my amazing friend! Today, we're diving deep into the world of analytics and insights. It's like having a chat with your business's data – understanding its story, what it loves and what it needs more of or less of.

So, let's turn these numbers into actionable strategies that lead to smashing success.

The Crucial Role of Analytics in Content Marketing

Picture analytics as your business' heartbeat monitor. It shows the health of your content and guides your decisions.

Stat Alert: According to a Forbes report, companies that use analytics are five times more likely to make faster decisions.

Why is this important?

Well, my friend, I'm so glad you asked. ;-)

The magic of making quick decisions in your business is super empowering. When you're able to snap up those decisions faster than a New York minute, some pretty amazing things start to happen. It's like giving your business a superpower. Here's why:

1. **Dance to the Beat of the Market:** Markets change faster than fashion trends, right? Being able to make quick decisions means you're always dancing in rhythm with those changes. It keeps your business fresh, relevant and oh-so-appealing.

2. **Boost Your Biz Efficiency:** Think of fast decision-making as your productivity turbo-boost. It's all about doing more in less time, and who doesn't want that? This way, you can focus on growing your dream without getting bogged down in the muck of indecision.

3. **Seize Those Sparkly Opportunities:** Ever seen those glittering business opportunities pop up? Well, fast decisions allow you to grab them before they disappear. It's like being the first in line at your favourite store's biggest sale of the year! WooHoo!

4. **Wave Goodbye to Stress:** Let's face it, dilly-dallying over decisions can be a major stress fest. Making decisions quickly, especially when they're backed

up by good old data, means less worrying and more doing. And that feels fantastic!

5. **Navigate the Bumpy Roads with Ease:** In business, sometimes you hit a bump *(or a giant pothole... I've sure found a few of those over the years!).* Being able to decide quickly helps you steer clear before things get too bumpy. It's like having an awesome GPS for your business journey.

6. **Be the Leader of the Pack:** Quick decision-making sets you apart from the crowd. It's your secret sauce for staying ahead of your competitors and positioning yourself as a leader in your industry. And who doesn't want to be leading the pack?

7. **Hello, Work-Life Harmony:** When you're not stuck in decision-making mode, guess what? You get more time for YOU. Whether it's family time, yoga or just binge-watching your favourite show, faster decisions free up precious moments for the things that light you up.

8. **Create a 'Can-Do' Culture:** Your decisiveness is contagious! It trickles down to your team, creating a vibrant, 'can-do' culture. Imagine a team that's all about action, not just deliberation. Pretty awesome, right?

So, my beautiful friend, let's embrace the power of fast, informed decision-making. It's not just about saving time; it's about elevating your entire business game.

And the best part?

It makes the entrepreneurial ride so much more exhilarating and fulfilling!

So, just how do we do this?

Mastering the Basics of Analytics

Let's start with the ABCs of analytics and what they mean for your content.

- **Acquisition Metrics:** Understand where your audience is coming from. For example, is it social media, organic search or referrals? And if it's social media – which platforms? If it's mostly from organic search, what keywords are they searching on to find you? Or if it's from referrals, who's referrals?
- **Behaviour Metrics:** Dive into what your audience does on your site. Which pages do they visit? How long do they stay?
- **Conversion Metrics:** These are your success stories. How many visitors are turning into subscribers or customers?

Deep Dive Example:

Imagine you own a boutique. You notice from Google Analytics that most of your traffic comes from Instagram. Almost no traffic is coming from Twitter. Knowing this, it's crystal clear where you should focus your marketing efforts!

Exploring Various Types of Analytics

There's a whole world of data waiting to be explored. Each type gives you different insights into your content strategy.

1. **Content Analytics:** Measure the performance of individual pieces of content. What's resonating with your audience?

2. **User Analytics:** Get to know your audience. What are their demographics, interests and online behaviours?

3. **Campaign Analytics:** Evaluate the success of specific marketing campaigns. Are they hitting the targets you've set?

Here's an Example:

Sophia runs a home décor blog. Through content analytics, she found that DIY articles are the most popular. This insight led her to focus more on DIY content, resulting in a 27% increase in engagement and 13.6% increase in sales to new customers.

Without any analytics to refer to, Sophia may never have known her audience resonate best with – and take more action from – her DIY articles.

Setting Goals and KPIs Like a Pro

Setting goals without data is like shooting arrows in the dark. Let's light it up with KPIs that matter.

- **SMART Goals:** Goals should be Specific, Measurable, Achievable, Relevant and Time-bound.
- **Custom KPIs:** Tailor your KPIs to match your unique business goals. It could be anything from download numbers for a lead magnet to engagement rates on Instagram posts.

Keep in mind that the of likes and followers you have isn't as relevant as the quality of them – e.g. if they're your ideal clients – or the actions they take. So don't get caught up in trying to get more likes and engagements without this then leading to more sales and better customer relationships.
SMART Goal Example:

Angela, a fitness coach, set a SMART goal to increase her YouTube subscribers by 20% in three months. She tracked her weekly subscriber growth as her KPI and adjusted her video content strategy accordingly.

She then checked in on her data regularly over the next 3 months and regularly adjusted her strategy further, depending on the stats. E.g. Doing more of what works and less of what doesn't.

The Art of Analysing and Interpreting Data

Interpreting data is like detective work. You're looking for clues in the numbers to solve the mystery of your audience's desires.

1. **Segment Your Data:** Break down your data. Look at different audience segments, time frames or content types.
2. **Look for Correlations:** Is there a link between the time you post and the engagement you receive?
3. **Contextualise Your Data:** Numbers don't exist in a vacuum. What was happening in your business or the world when you saw spikes or drops?

In-Depth Data Interpretation:
Marco, who owns a coffee shop, noticed a spike in website traffic during a local festival. He capitalised on this by running a targeted campaign during similar events, increasing his sales substantially. Plus, he was then able to turn many of these new customers into repeat customers.

Avoiding Common Analytics Pitfalls

Even seasoned marketers can stumble in the analytics game. Let's navigate these common pitfalls.

- **Analysis Paralysis:** Too much data can be overwhelming. Focus on a few key metrics that align with your goals.
- **Chasing Vanity Metrics:** Likes and shares feel good, but do they align with your business goals? Focus on metrics that drive action.
- **Ignoring the Story Behind the Data:** Numbers are just the surface. Dive deeper to understand the why behind the trends.

Leveraging Tools and Resources

There's a tool for every analytics need. Here's how to pick the right one for you.

- **Choosing the Right Tools:** Look for tools that align with your goals. Do you need detailed website analytics or are you more focused on social media?
- **Combining Tools for a Holistic View:** Sometimes, one tool isn't enough. Use a combination to get a full picture of your content's performance.

Tools Example:

Carla, a fashion blogger, uses Google Analytics for website data, Instagram Insights for her social media engagement and Kartra for email campaign analytics. This trio gives her a comprehensive understanding of her overall content performance.

Wrapping Up with Actionable Insights

Remember, analytics is not just about numbers; it's about stories, trends and insights. It's a powerful tool to help you make informed decisions and skyrocket your content's success.

Your Next Step: Choose one aspect of your content – maybe it's your blog, a social media channel or your email marketing. Set a specific goal and identify which KPIs will help you measure success. Start tracking, interpreting and let the insights guide your way to success.

In Chapter 15, we delve into the art of *Harnessing the Power of Content Repurposing*. We'll explore how you can take a single piece of content and spin it into multiple, impactful pieces for different platforms.

It's all about maximising your content's reach and effectiveness with smart, creative strategies. So, get ready to give your content a glamorous makeover, darling!

Chapter 15: Harnessing The Power Of Content Repurposing

Maximising Every Piece of Content You Create

Hello, Gorgeous! Are you ready to get the most out of every blog post, video and podcast you create?

Today, we're diving into the goldmine of content repurposing. Imagine turning one piece of content into a treasure trove of opportunities. Let's get started on this exciting journey... because the sooner you start doing this, the sooner you can grab more time back for doing things you love doing!

The Magic of Content Repurposing

Content repurposing isn't just a tactic; it's an art. It's about taking your hard work and giving it new life, new formats and new audiences. And it's about working smart – making the most of what you have.

Eye-Opening Stat: A study by Social Media Today suggests that repurposing content can boost your traffic by up to 300%. That's transforming your single seed of content into a beautiful garden of opportunities!

Why Repurpose Your Content?

1. **Reach and Engage New Audiences:** Your audience is diverse, and they consume content in different ways. Repurposing helps you meet them on their favourite platforms.

2. **Reinforce and Amplify Your Message:** The Rule of Seven in marketing says that people need to hear your message several times before they take action. By repurposing, you're echoing your message across the digital landscape.

3. **Save Time and Boost Efficiency:** Creating quality content is time-consuming. Repurposing it in various formats makes your content strategy more efficient and effective.

Transforming Content into Multiple Formats

Let's look at how you can creatively repurpose content across different mediums.

1. **Blog Posts to Podcasts:** Take your most popular blog posts and turn them into podcast episodes. It's like inviting

your audience to a personal chat where you delve deeper into the topics.

2. **Webinar to Video Clips:** Got a great webinar? Break it down into short, informative video clips. These are perfect for sharing on social media or as part of an email series.

3. **Infographics from Data-Heavy Content:** Turn your research or data-driven blog posts into visually appealing infographics. They're perfect for Pinterest and Instagram and great for visual learners.

4. **Social Media Goldmine:** Almost every piece of content can be transformed into engaging social media posts. Think bite-sized tips, inspiring quotes, quick how-to videos and eye-catching graphics.

In-Depth Example:

Laura, a digital marketing specialist, hosted a successful webinar on SEO strategies. She repurposed it into a series of YouTube video tutorials, a series of detailed blog posts and several infographics highlighting key points, which she then shared on LinkedIn and Facebook. Then she had the webinar transcribed and created a PDF ebook from it, which she offered as an incentive for people to opt-in to her list. And of course, she emailed her subscribers to make sure they had all this juicy info too. All from one webinar!

The Strategy Behind Effective Content Repurposing

To make the most out of repurposing, you need a thoughtful approach.

1. **Identify Your Best-Performing Content:** Use analytics to find out which pieces of content resonated the most with your audience. These are your repurposing goldmines.

2. **Match Content to Platform Needs:** Understand the nuances of each platform. What works on Instagram might not work on LinkedIn. Tailor your repurposed content to fit.

3. **Maintain Consistency in Brand Voice:** Ensure all repurposed content still sounds unmistakably like you. Consistency strengthens your brand identity.

Strategy Spotlight:

James, a personal finance advisor, noticed his blog post about budgeting tips was his most-read piece. He repurposed it into an infographic, a series of tweets and even a short TikTok series. Each platform got a tailored piece of the content puzzle, expanding his reach significantly. He could take this even further, but this is a good start.

Navigating the Challenges of Content Repurposing

Content repurposing is powerful, but it's not without challenges.

- **Freshness Over Repetition:** It's crucial to add new insights or perspectives to make the repurposed content feel fresh and valuable. But at the same time, don't worry about sounding a little repetitive. Remember, different people will see your content on different platforms and will learn more from seeing it multiple times.
- **Quality Control:** Ensure that every repurposed piece maintains the high quality your audience expects. It's not just about changing the format; it's about enhancing the value.

Tracking the Impact of Repurposed Content

Understanding the effectiveness of your repurposed content is key to refining your strategy.

- **Define Clear Metrics:** Depending on your goals *(increased engagement,*

higher traffic, lead generation), set specific metrics to track the performance of each repurposed piece.
- **Use Analytics Tools:** Use tools like Google Analytics for your website, native analytics on social platforms and email campaign tools to track engagement and conversion.

Success Measurement Example:

Katie, a freelance writer, turned her popular article on productivity tips into a series of Instagram posts and an email newsletter series. By tracking the engagement and click-through rates, she found a 42% increase in newsletter sign-ups and a significant boost in Instagram engagement.

Leveraging Tools for Repurposing

To streamline your repurposing process, tap into the power of various tools.
- **Content Management Tools:** Plan and organise your repurposing strategy using tools like Asana or Trello. *(I use Trello a LOT, but Asana is also very good.)*
- **Design Software:** Canva and Adobe Spark are great for creating visually appealing social media posts, infographics and more. *(I use and love*

Canva.com. I chose to upgrade to the paid version, but the free version is great too if you're on a tight budget.)

Wrapping Up and Next Steps

Repurposing content is all about spreading your wisdom far and wide. It's a smart way to maximise your impact and connect with more people without reinventing the wheel.

Your Next Step: Review your content library. Pick a piece that resonated with your audience and brainstorm different ways to repurpose it for various platforms. Remember, each piece of content is a seed that can grow into a beautiful bouquet of engaging material.

Ready for more insights?

I hope so, because in the next chapter, ***Content Planning and Calendars: Organising for Consistency***, we'll discuss developing a strategic content calendar for long-term engagement and impact. Plus, it makes it soooo much easier for you to stay on top of your content creation!

Chapter 16: Content Planning and Calendars: Organising for Consistency

Developing a Strategic Content Calendar for Sustained Engagement and Impact

Hey there, content creator extraordinaire! Today, we're going to deep-dive into the intricacies of Content Planning and Calendars.

Think of it as the heart of your content strategy – a compass that guides your every move and keeps your audience enchanted.

So, let's roll up our sleeves and unravel the magic behind crafting a content calendar that not only keeps you organised but also captivates your audience consistently.

The Magic of Content Planning

1. Why Plan? Unveiling the Benefits
A Blueprint for Success
Content planning isn't just about scheduling dates on a calendar; it's your strategic blueprint for success. It provides a roadmap, ensuring that every piece of content contributes meaningfully to your overarching goals. Imagine building a

castle without a blueprint – it might look impressive, but it won't stand the test of time.

Example: Look at successful brands: they don't randomly post content. Each piece is strategically planned to align with their brand story and business objectives.

2. Consistency Is Key: The Engagement Enchantment
Building Trust Through Regularity

Consistency is your magic wand when it comes to engagement. Your audience craves regularity – it builds a sense of trust and reliability. Just like your favourite TV show airing at the same time each week, consistent content keeps your brand on the forefront of your audience's minds.

Example: Think of brands like Apple or Nike. Their consistent content rhythm ensures that consumers are always anticipating what comes next.

Crafting Your Content Calendar

1. Aligning with Business Goals
Your Calendar, Your Goals

Every content piece should be a step toward your business goals. If your goal is to increase brand awareness, plan content that introduces your brand to new audiences. Aligning your calendar with your goals ensures that every piece of content serves a purpose.

Example: If your goal is to boost product sales, plan content that highlights product features, benefits and customer testimonials. Anticipate questions and objections prospects may have at this stage and answer them within your content where possible.

2. Understanding Your Audience: The Audience Alchemy
Creating Content Your Audience Craves

Understanding your audience is like having a magic potion. Use analytics and social listening to uncover their preferences. If they love bite-sized video content, incorporate more videos into your calendar. The key is to create content that speaks directly to their needs and desires.

Example: If your audience engages more with behind-the-scenes content, plan regular "day in the life" posts or behind-the-scenes videos.

3. Mapping Content Types: The Variety Spell
A Feast for Every Palate

Variety keeps your content calendar interesting. Map out different content types, such as blog posts, videos, infographics and podcasts, to cater to different preferences. Like a delicious buffet, your content calendar should offer a diverse menu to keep your audience engaged.

Example: If you've been predominantly using blog posts, try incorporating video content or infographics to add variety.

4. The Editorial Calendar Dance: Weekly, Monthly and Beyond
Setting the Rhythm

The frequency of your content matters. Whether you choose to publish weekly, bi-weekly or monthly, set a rhythm that aligns with your audience's expectations. Consistency in both frequency and quality is the key to keeping your audience engaged.

Example: If you're a small business, starting with bi-weekly blog posts and monthly videos can be a manageable and effective rhythm. If you can manage a weekly blog post, even better. However, aim for consistency.

5. Seasonal and Trend Magic: Riding the Waves
Surfing the Trends

Infuse your calendar with the magic of seasons and trends. Stay aware of industry trends and create content that aligns with what's current. Seasonal content adds relevance and keeps your calendar dynamic and engaging.

Example: If you're in the fitness industry, planning content around New Year's resolutions or summer body goals aligns with seasonal trends.

Tools of the Trade: Content Calendar Platforms

1. Google Calendar: The Classic Charm
Simple and Effective
Google Calendar's simplicity is its charm. Colour-code content types and easily visualise your content landscape. It's a classic choice for those starting out.

Example: Assign different colours to blog posts, videos and social media posts to easily distinguish content types.

2. Trello: The Visual Vision
Kanban Magic
Trello offers a visual approach to content planning. Organise your content like a series of cards, moving them through different stages. It's a visual delight that adds creativity to your planning process.

Example: Use Trello boards for different content stages – ideas, in progress, published – to track content status at a glance.

3. CoSchedule.com: The All-in-One Ally
Streamlined Bliss
CoSchedule.com is an all-in-one solution, combining content planning, social media scheduling and team collaboration. Streamline your workflow and ensure everything is in sync.

Example: Use CoSchedule's social media scheduling feature to plan and automate posts promoting your content across platforms.

The Lifecycle of Content

1. Creation: Conjuring Compelling Creations
The Artistic Alchemy

During the creation phase, focus on crafting compelling content. Each piece should be a work of art – informative, entertaining or both. Consider your audience's journey and create content that guides them seamlessly from awareness to action.

Example: If you're creating a blog post, incorporate engaging visuals, storytelling and a clear call-to-action to encourage reader interaction.

2. Distribution: The Social Symphony
Spreading the Magic

Content distribution is where the social symphony plays. Use your calendar to schedule social media posts that amplify your content. Leverage different platforms and formats to ensure your content reaches its full potential.

Example: If you've created a podcast episode, plan corresponding social media posts with snippets, quotes and behind-the-scenes content to promote it.

3. Analysis: The Crystal Ball Gazing
Learning from Insights
After your content is out in the world, turn to analytics as your crystal ball. Track performance metrics – engagement, conversions, click-through rates. Learn from the insights and let them guide future content decisions.

Example: If a particular blog post receives high engagement, consider creating a follow-up post or expanding on the topic in other content formats.

Content Calendar Maintenance

1. Regular Audits: Keeping the Magic Alive
Ensuring Relevance
Your content calendar is a living entity. Conduct regular audits to ensure content is still relevant and aligns with evolving business goals. Prune away the irrelevant and make room for fresh blooms.

Example: If a planned series of posts isn't resonating with your audience, be open to pivoting and adjusting your content plan.

2. Flexibility: The Adaptation Spell
Embracing Change
While consistency is key, flexibility is the adaptation spell. Be open to adjusting your calendar based on unforeseen events, industry shifts or audience feedback. A flexible approach

ensures your content stays nimble and responsive.

Example: If a social media trend becomes prominent, adjust your content calendar to incorporate relevant content quickly.

Your Content Symphony

Congratulations, content virtuoso! You've crafted a content calendar that's not just a schedule; it's a symphony of strategic planning, audience understanding and creative magic.

As we end this chapter, remember that your calendar is a living, breathing entity. Keep it vibrant, adapt when needed and let it guide your content journey towards sustained engagement and impact.

In the next chapter, we're going to tackle a topic close to my heart: keeping your creative spark alive while maintaining a healthy balance in your work and personal life. Because, my beautiful friend, you can't pour from an empty cup.

So, stay tuned for some game-changing strategies to keep you at your creative best!

Chapter 17: Overcoming Content Burnout: Self-Care Strategies for Creators

Addressing the Challenges of Content Creation and Maintaining a Healthy Work-Life Balance

Hello, wonderful creator! It's time for a heart-to-heart about a topic that's vital yet often overlooked in our entrepreneurial journey – burnout.

As business owners, we're constantly juggling various roles and it's all too easy to lose ourselves in the endless cycle of 'stuff' that needs to be done. Then we add in a handful of guilt because we're not spending enough time with our family or our friends or maintaining our home. All too often, we're constantly beating ourselves up because we're not living that perfectly balanced life that we seem to think every successful person is living.

So, let's settle in with our favourite drink and explore how we can keep our creative flames burning brightly without burning out.

Understanding Content Burnout

Think of content burnout as a creative drought, where motivation and inspiration seem to have dried up. It's a state where the demands of constant content creation become more of a burden than a joy.

The Stats Speak:
According to a study by the Content Marketing Institute, a staggering 70% of content creators report experiencing burnout at some stage. This isn't just an occasional 'off day'; it's a widespread issue in the industry.

Recognising the Signs of Burnout:
It's crucial to identify burnout early on. Here are some telltale signs that you might be experiencing burnout:

- **Chronic Fatigue:** Feeling consistently tired, not just physically, but mentally drained. This isn't the usual end-of-day weariness; it's a deep-rooted exhaustion that doesn't go away with a good night's sleep.
- **Creative Block:** Finding it increasingly difficult to come up with new ideas or feeling like your well of creativity has dried up.
- **Lack of Satisfaction:** Experiencing a sense of dissatisfaction or

underachievement with the content you produce, regardless of its success or quality.

- **Irritability and Frustration:** Feeling easily annoyed or overwhelmed by small issues, and a general sense of frustration with your content creation process.
- **Decreased Motivation:** Losing the drive and enthusiasm that you once had for creating content, even for topics you're passionate about.
- **Avoidance Behaviour:** Procrastinating more than usual or finding excuses to avoid working on content-related tasks.
- **Imposter Syndrome:** Doubting your skills and accomplishments as a content creator, feeling like a fraud despite evidence of your capabilities.

Recognising these signs is the first step in addressing and overcoming content burnout. It's about being honest with yourself and acknowledging when things aren't quite right. Remember, acknowledging burnout isn't a sign of weakness; it's an act of self-awareness and strength.

Digging Deeper into the Causes of Burnout

It's crucial to understand what's fuelling your burnout so you can address it effectively.

1. **Unrealistic Expectations:** Setting the bar too high can lead to constant feelings of inadequacy.
2. **Lack of Boundaries:** Blurring the lines between work and personal life can lead to overwork and stress.
3. **Social Media Pressure:** The need to constantly be 'on' and engaging can be exhausting.
4. **Perfectionism Trap:** Striving for perfection in every piece of content can be paralysing.

Strategies to Prevent and Overcome Content Burnout

Let's look at more ways to tackle this issue head-on:

1. **Mindful Scheduling:** Prioritise your tasks and recognise the power of saying 'no' to avoid overcommitment.
2. **Regular Check-ins:** Periodically assess your workload and stress levels. Are you pushing too hard?

3. **Creative Exercises:** Engage in activities unrelated to your work to spark creativity.

4. **Stay Inspired:** Regularly consume content that motivates and inspires you, but also gives you a break from your niche.

More Real-Life Examples:

- Linda, a digital marketer, started scheduling 'no-work' weekends which allowed her to return to work refreshed and full of ideas.
- Rachel, a writer, began practicing yoga and found that it not only relieved stress but also opened up a new wellspring of creativity.
- Personally, I've found daily exercise, yoga, meditation and 'fun' have been my saviours. Those, and learning not to push myself too hard and to set – and adhere to – strict boundaries in various areas of my life. It didn't happen overnight, but I found these things helped day by day.

Balancing Creativity and Productivity

The key to sustainable content creation lies in finding a balance where productivity and creativity coexist harmoniously.

Deep Dive into Balancing Techniques:
- **Creative Rituals:** Establish rituals that signal to your brain that it's time to get creative.
- **Productivity Techniques:** Explore methods like the Pomodoro Technique to improve focus during work periods.
- **Creative Playtime:** Allocate time for unstructured creative activities that are just for fun.

Extended Example:

Kevin, a podcaster, sets aside Friday afternoons for creative brainstorming sessions with no agenda, which often leads to his best ideas.

Personally, I get my best ideas while walking, preferably along the beach, or while sitting at a café or park after a long beach walk. So, it's important for me to carry a notebook and pens, just in case. Or recording your thoughts on your phone can work too.

The Art of Delegating and Outsourcing

It's not only about working smarter; sometimes, it's about knowing when to hand over the reins.

In-Depth on Delegation:
- **Identify Your Strengths:** Focus on what you do best and delegate the rest.

- **Building a Trusted Team:** Investing time in training a team can pay off in the long run.
- **Letting Go:** Trust your team with responsibilities and resist the urge to micromanage.

Delegation Success Story Expanded:

Kate, an online coach, hired a content writer and a social media manager, which not only reduced her workload but also brought fresh perspectives to her brand. Her content writer specialises in this area and invests in on-going training, keeping up to date with the latest tools and trends. This means Kate not only gets great quality content, but she's also freeing up so much of her time.

Technology: A Creator's Best Friend

Leveraging technology can drastically reduce the stress associated with content creation.

Exploring More Tech Tools:

- **Content Creation Tools:** Explore tools like Grammarly.com for writing or Canva.com for design to streamline your creation process.
- **AI:** There are so many AI *(Artificial Intelligence)* tools on the market and more and more coming out all the time. I don't recommend relying on these tools

to take over all of your content marketing, however they can be great for helping you to research your ideal client or brainstorm content ideas.

- **Digital Detox:** While technology plays an important role in helping you create and manage your content marketing, it's also important to switch off. Periodically unplugging from digital devices can help in mental rejuvenation.

Building a Support Network: More than Just Networking

Creating a circle of support is about building relationships that offer mutual understanding and encouragement.

Expanding Your Support Network:

- **Delegate:** Delegate any tasks that aren't part of your 'zone of genius' – these are the things that you do best. These team members can be a great form of support for you and your business.
- **Mentorship:** Seek mentors who can provide guidance and support.
- **Accountability Partners:** Team up with someone who can keep you accountable in your goals and self-care practices.

Networking Impact:

Sophia, a lifestyle blogger, found that regular online catchups with her mentor provided invaluable insights and emotional support, crucial for her well-being. Plus, it helped to keep her motivated and accountable.

Wrapping Up and Looking Ahead

As we wrap up this chapter, remember that taking care of yourself isn't a luxury; it's a necessity for sustainable creativity and success. Start implementing these strategies and watch as your content and well-being flourish together.

Your Next Step: Take a moment to write down one self-care practice and one strategy to reduce burnout that you will start implementing this week. Remember, small steps lead to big changes!

Chapter 18: Your Ongoing Content Journey

Hey there, my beautiful friend! Can you believe we've journeyed together through this entire book?

It's been an absolute pleasure sharing insights, strategies and stories with you, as if we've been sipping our favourite drinks and having a cozy chat, perhaps with a little sweet treat alongside.

I hope you've felt me right there with you, supporting your content marketing endeavours every step of the way and cheering you on.

As we reach the end of our content marketing adventure, it's time to reflect on all that we've learned and, more importantly, how you can continue to grow and innovate in your content marketing journey. Because remember, this isn't a final destination – it's the beginning of your remarkable content marketing story.

Let's take a moment to recap the key takeaways that will serve as your guideposts on this ongoing journey:

We started by laying a strong foundation, clarifying your brand, audience and goals. Remember, it's not about trying to be everywhere; it's about being where your ideal audience hangs out. By understanding your target market and choosing a platform that resonates with them, you'll be off to a strong start.

Together, we delved into the art of storytelling and the importance of creating content that not only educates but also entertains and inspires. Your stories have the power to connect with your audience on a deep level, so don't shy away from sharing your experiences, lessons and victories.

Mapping Your Path

Content marketing without a strategy is like setting sail without a compass. We explored the significance of planning, setting goals and creating a content calendar. A well-thought-out strategy will keep you on course and ensure that every piece of content serves a purpose in your larger narrative.

Mastering Social Media

Social media can be a whirlwind, but remember the wise words from this proverb, *"If you chase two rabbits, you will not catch either one."* This adage applies perfectly to your social media strategy. It reminds us that it's not about being everywhere; it's about being where it matters most.

In the world of content marketing and social media, trying to be on every platform and chasing after every trend can lead to scattered efforts and diluted impact. Instead, our focus should be on narrowing down our choices and dedicating our energy to one or two platforms that align most closely with our target audience.

Why is this so crucial?

Well, when you spread yourself too thin, you risk missing the chance to build meaningful connections. By focusing your efforts strategically, you can engage more deeply and authentically with your community. It's about quality over quantity.

So, think about where your ideal audience hangs out, choose the platforms that resonate with them the most and pour your heart and soul into creating valuable content for those select channels. This way, you'll not only catch the rabbits *(metaphorically speaking, of course... I don't actually condone going out catching, or even chasing, rabbits!)* but also nurture and grow a thriving online presence.

The Missing Link

Remember, creating content is only half the fun; promoting it is the other crucial piece of the puzzle. As we discussed in the promotion section, consistency and perseverance are key.

Keep sharing your content and exploring new promotion strategies, and before long you'll see that snowball effect in action.

Going Beyond

In the advanced section, we delved into analytics, content repurposing, planning and one of the most important parts – self-care.

These are the tools and practices that will help you take your content marketing to the next level.

Remember to measure your success, repurpose your content for maximum impact *(with minimal effort... yes please!)* and prioritise self-care to fuel your creativity.

Your Toolkit

And then, please don't forget the valuable resources available to support your journey, from tools and recommended reading to additional wisdom shared. A link to a list of my recommended resources is included in the final chapter, which follows this one. Building a toolkit and staying curious will keep your skills sharp.

So, here's the thing, my dear friend: this isn't the end. It's a mere pause in our conversation. I'm excited about the future and all the incredible content marketing adventures that await you. There's always room to grow, innovate and refine your strategies. Keep learning, keep experimenting, and most importantly, keep being your beautiful, authentic self.

In the world of content marketing, there are no limits to what you can achieve. Your unique voice and stories have the power to touch hearts, inspire change and drive your business forward. It's not always easy, but it's undoubtedly rewarding.

As we wrap up this book, I want you to know that I'm cheering you on from the sidelines, celebrating your successes and here to support you whenever you need it. I can't wait for our next cozy chat about your business growth, your triumphs and your journey into the exciting world of content marketing!

I'd be over the moon if you could spare a moment to leave an honest review on Amazon. I'm so grateful you're here and your thoughts mean the world to me. Plus, they help other fabulous people discover my books. And hey, if you feel like sharing, visit me online at www.facebook.com/DonnaMarieCoggins. I'm all ears for your favourite chapter and the ideas you've brought to life from my book. Your support and insights are what keep this journey so exciting!

Thank you for sharing this time with me. Until we meet again, keep radiating your content marketing magic out into the world. Your brilliance is boundless and your impact immeasurable.

With all my warmth and support,
Donna-Marie xx

Chapter 19: Resources And Bonuses

I initially thought I'd kick off this chapter by giving you a treasure trove of resources to up your content marketing game. Because let's face it, the right tools can make your content marketing journey not just more effective, but also a whole lot more fun!

But here's the thing – the internet is always evolving. Tools and websites change overnight. So, rather than giving you a static list that might become outdated by the time you flip to this page, I've got something better! I've created a special Resources page on my website, just for you. It's a dynamic, ever-evolving space where you'll find all the latest and greatest tools and links. Check it out at: www.donna-mariecoggins.com/business-resources

This page is my labour of love, constantly updated to ensure you have access to the newest resources. Plus, I'll keep adding more gems as I discover and vet them myself – only the best for you!

And guess what? I've got some bonus gifts for you too – just because you're amazing. You can grab these goodies at: www.donna-mariecoggins.com/bonuses.
Consider it a little 'thank you' for joining me on this exciting journey! :-) ❤

About The Author:

Meet Donna-Marie Coggins, also known as DM, a dynamic author, entrepreneur and online mentor from Queensland, Australia. With over two decades of experience, DM leads her multi-award-winning venture, Jacaranda Business Support Services, blending business success with personal well-being.  She's not just a content marketing specialist; she's a guiding light, helping people craft a business that brings joy and fulfillment, aligning professional achievements with a life by design.

DM believes in the magic of merging simplicity with big dreams in business. Her mission is to empower you to tailor your business to your unique strengths, aligning it with the lifestyle you desire.

Celebrated in the "Who's Who of Australian Women," Donna-Marie radiates positivity and is dedicated to uplifting others. She's more than a teacher; she's a testament to the power of effective digital marketing, particularly for small business owners and solopreneurs.

Donna-Marie warmly welcomes those who share her vision of a balanced life and professional success. If her philosophy resonates with you and you'd like to learn more about Donna-Marie, you can connect with her at:

Donna-MarieCoggins.com
Facebook.com/DonnaMarieCoggins